My Life and
My Death

My Life and My Death

A PRIEST CONFRONTS
HIS CANCER

Jeffrey T. Simmons

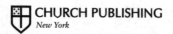

Cataloging-in-Publication Data is available from
the Library of Congress

ISBN 0-89869-445-0

Church Publishing Incorporated
445 Fifth Avenue
New York, NY 10016
www.churchpublishing.org

5 4 3 2 1

Contents

Foreword

Steve Simmons

In my family, we have never had much use for death, although we seem to do as much of it as anybody else. Our motto could well be, in the words of Edna St. Vincent Millay, "I shall die, but that is all that I shall do for death. I am not on his payroll." But when we finally do get down to death, we do it rather well. Although my mother wasn't given such a chance (her sudden death begins the story you are about to read), my beloved Aunt Jinny was. She used the opportunity to invite her nephews and nieces to her house one day, pour us all a glass of sherry, divvy her most valued possessions among us, mark them with one of those pistol-grip label makers, and pronounce with satisfaction, "There. That's done," confident that her things would go to loving homes after her departure. Others appear to have drawn strength from this matter-of-fact attitude toward eternity as well. The day before her death, as I sat by her hospital bed, several staff members dropped by and asked me if they could have a moment alone with her. They evidently needed a last word of counsel and, perhaps, of blessing from this dying patient who had become their friend and mentor.

Several months later, our dad held court from his hospital bed on the day of his death, with physicians and attorneys in attendance, gently telling my stepmother, then in the early stages of Alzheimer's, that he had arranged for her care at a retirement home two blocks from their house.

Then it was my brother Jeff's turn. In true form, he turned his cancer diagnosis into an opportunity by turning on his laptop and seeing how he could make some sense of his experience both for himself and for fellow travelers. Not that he was cavalier about it; he rued the fact that, having attended his son Matt's wedding only about a month before his death, he would not live to see his grandchildren. He hated facing the prospect of leaving his wife, Beverly. Their friends had often said that the two of them were the "most married" people they'd ever known. But, things being what they were, he determined to put even his dying to good use.

The weekend he died (at home, fortunately, in the care of some wonderful folks from hospice), I took a few moments away from his bedside to stroll the grounds of St. Mary's Convent in Peekskill, New York, where Jeff, an Episcopal priest, was the spiritual director. I wandered by the pen where some goats were being kept as a welcoming gesture to several nuns from Malawi, and found one of the sisters feeding the animals. As we talked, I mentioned the curious fact that, even though the hospice personnel had installed a stationary oxygen concentrator by his bed to help him breathe, there was a freestanding oxygen bottle on wheels in a corner of the dining room. She smiled and told me that, sick as he was, he had planned to lead a conference on spirituality and healing at a nearby church two weeks earlier, but had had to go to the hospital instead. "He had transportation worked out and everything. You know how cowboys always say they want to die with their boots on? Jeff wanted to die laying his hands on other people, to heal them."

That was my brother; and it has been an honor for me to help edit his book. With this memoir, he has given us who knew and loved him an inestimable gift; for we can say that we know his mind during the time when he was preparing to take his leave of us. I hope that you, too, will find these words of comfort and encouragement, especially if you find yourself walking through the valley of the shadow of death; for he meant them for you most of all. Thanks especially to my sister-in-law Beverly, who traveled this way with him and whose help has been invaluable in preparing this manuscript for publication; and to Johnny Ross of Church Publishing, who has been a model of tact and discernment in piloting a novice through the shoals of making a deeply personal series of reflections fit for a wider reading public.

This one's for you, brother.

☙ Introit ❧

June 1969

To call my one-room apartment on the Lower East Side of Manhattan a "bachelor pad" would be far too kind. It had all the uncouthness associated with bachelors, especially bachelors just out of college with no money, but none of the romantic elegance of a "pad." Still, I was proud to have put together a rough parody of a furnished room for almost nothing. A bookshelf of bricks and unfinished pine boards flanked a desk made of a door propped on cardboard boxes. A second-hand mattress bought at one of the less disreputable-looking furniture outlets in the area was comfortable enough flat on the floor, and so far the cockroaches had been so content under the stove that they hadn't expanded their territory to come anywhere near it. I had a roommate a month before who had sort of gone mad and started smashing every cockroach he saw with the heel of his shoe. It was a useless gesture, and he eventually moved out.

I was already enrolled as a divinity student at Union Seminary, but when they had offered a new "Urban

Intern" program, basically a year of living in the city and learning about "real life," I jumped at it. There was also the promise that we would be studying how to bring about "social change in the city." This was only a few years after the Protestant denominations had become seriously involved in politics and social action, and in my enthusiasm (hey, I had already marched with Martin Luther King in Selma, Alabama) I was a willing recruit. Somehow eating my dinner on a table made of cardboard boxes fit the image.

The phone call came late on a Sunday afternoon. My dad told me, in a strangely unemotional voice, that my mom had just died of a heart attack, and that he needed me to come home.

At times like this, you don't feel; you just act. I had to get an airline ticket. Unfortunately my finances were as primordial as my furniture. I had about twenty dollars in my pocket and a few hundred in my checkbook, and even I wasn't naïve enough to think I could get a check cashed in Manhattan on a Sunday afternoon.

I don't remember any of the details of how I got home, except that some friends from my church bailed me out. From then on it was the usual dreary ritual of death, made even drearier by my mother's recent medical history. For the last seven years, she had been virtually bedridden and in constant pain from a back ailment that had baffled the doctors. At one point during my summer vacation, she had had a virtual (although blessedly temporary) psychotic break brought on by the pain medication, and I once had to physically stop her from committing suicide right in front of me. When she died, we all agreed that, given the hopelessness of her situation, it was probably a good thing.

My father, my brother, and I all went through periods of raging against God. Our family was too solidly Presbyterian to deny his existence outright, and besides, that wouldn't have served the emotional need. If God didn't exist, there would be no one to get mad at, and that would have been too painful. We each needed a villain, a target for our sense of grievance, and like so many people I have known through the years, we elected God.

I had become hooked on French existentialism, especially the writings of Albert Camus, during my junior year in France, and that lent a certain self-conscious sophistication to my anger at God. *La Peste*, Camus' dreary story of the plague devastating a city in North Africa, gave perfect expression to what I was feeling, especially the part where a good-hearted but bumbling priest, Father Paneloux, is trying to explain the problem of evil. This provokes a magnificent temper tantrum from the town doctor, Bernard Rieux, who has exhausted himself in a futile effort to control the plague.

"It's true," Rieux said, "excuse me. Fatigue is a kind of madness. But it has been many hours in this city since I have felt anything but my revulsion."

"I understand," murmured Paneloux. "It is revolting because it is beyond us. But maybe we have to love what we cannot understand."

Rieux straightened up in one violent movement. He regarded Paneloux with all the force and passion of which he was capable, and shook his head.

"No, Father," he said, "I have another idea of love. And I will refuse to the death to love this creation where children are tortured."

Astonishingly, I still have my copy of _La Peste_. Holding it fills me with a kind of bittersweet affection. The depressed-looking photo of Camus on the back holding his cigarette Humphrey-Bogart-style brings back memories of a kind of artsy French melancholy that shouldn't be pleasant, but somehow is. I am tempted to write it off as a particularly elegant excuse for self-pity, but I think it is more than that. Camus is saying something that in the depths of my soul I desperately needed to say too.

I know how it can be perversely pleasant to carry a grudge against God. I became a master at asking, "Why?" — not in the sense that I was honestly looking for an answer, but more as an accusation, a rhetorical device that assumes there is no "why" and that God is guilty of an inexcusable injustice.

Looking back, I am a bit amazed at the questions I was not asking. In my experience almost nobody who is carrying resentment against God asks these questions, although they now seem to me inescapable. I was making that question of evil almost an emotional parlor game, when I was actually toying with a nightmare of unbearable proportions. I never asked the question, "If God is capable of brutal, apparently meaningless evil, and if I am totally under the power of that God and no other for the rest of eternity, then what kind of future am I headed for?" If I make God into a devil, then I have to look forward to the devil's company for all eternity. You would think that would make people pause before they start vilifying God, but somehow it never seems to.

It is possible to come to a place where you don't want God to be good. C. S. Lewis calls it "the sulks." It carries a heady sense of power, as though I am standing above God, throwing lightning bolts of condemnation on him, as though I was some kind of Master of the Universe. I think God in his love indulgently tolerates this in his children for a while. I have known people for whom this sulking became at least semipermanent. This is truly the front porch of hell.

I wasn't allowed to get that far. By the end of about a year I was starting to run out of steam. As the resentment receded it was replaced, I don't know how, by a subtle, almost imperceptible sense that everything was all right after all. I had spent a year consciously refusing to love what I couldn't understand, but that thing I couldn't understand was coming in the back door of my mind and loving me. My resentments were not so much defeated by argument as eroded away by a mysterious gentleness.

This book is about that gentleness. Anyone looking for an irrefutable argument for the goodness of God will be disappointed. But I am writing this in the hope that many will come to see "the sulks" as the dead end it is and take as a new working hypothesis that, if we look for the goodness of God, even in tragic situations like cancer, we will find that he is far better than we dared hope.

This book is based on my belief that God's love is far stronger, warmer, safer, and more reliable than any of us but the great saints even suspect. It is what all of our hearts actually long for. It is the meeting of our deepest needs and the fulfilling of our wildest desires.

I believe, and I believe Jesus taught insistently, that there is no theoretical limit to how close God wants to come to us or how intensely we can experience his presence and fatherly care. In a difficult time, such as serious illness, it can make the difference between heaven and hell, life or death.

The reason so few people experience God's love in any depth is not in any way God's fault. The problem is the skill, energy, and tragic stubbornness we put into running away from him. We have been doing it so long and so well that we usually are totally unaware of it.

The solution is simply to learn to trust God. But I am talking about a radical trust, a trust so deep and total that after twenty-eight years of ordained ministry I am only now starting to realize what I have been talking about. But I am starting to see, as though I am just making out something in the distant horizon, what that kind of trust can be and what unimagined benefits go with it. Now I am learning to say with St. Augustine:

> You shed your fragrance and I drew in my breath and I pant for you. I tasted and now I hunger and thirst. You touched me and now I burn with longing for your peace.
>
> — *The Confessions*

My greatest teacher has been my cancer.

One

The First Surgery

My medical adventure began in November 2000, when I perforated my intestine. I had thought I had a stomach flu, but instead of putting me on an antibiotic, the doctor sent me to a surgeon, who sent me to the emergency room. The surgeon ordered blood work, an X-ray and CAT scan, but when the X-ray showed a pool of air in the top of the abdominal cavity, he told his assistant, "There is no time for a CAT scan. We will just have to deal with whatever we find when we get in." His face was grim.

The surgeon went off to prepare to operate. I handed Beverly my Palm Pilot and asked her to get people praying for me. She went off to make calls, and I was left alone on a stretcher in the emergency room.

I know what I am going to say next will inspire a lot of skepticism, but the only way I can think to say what happened is just to say it.

Jesus walked in the door.

John Henry Newman, when describing an early religious experience, said it was "something of which I am still more certain than that I have hands and feet." That night, I knew that kind of certainty. Nothing will ever convince me that this wasn't real.

I didn't see or hear anything, no words were used, but what I felt was intense. Unfortunately, the feeling can only be described with words that have become so trivialized that they no longer have the power I need.

I felt loved. That says everything, and nothing. I now understand how a love can be so wonderful that one would sell everything one had if that is what it cost. To be loved by Jesus, accepted with no trace of criticism, offered a safe place where nothing is demanded, and all of my deepest needs are understood without my needing to say anything. To really start to believe that he is enjoying being with you is something I never experienced before.

I felt safe. I had no idea if I was going to survive the night or not, but somehow it didn't matter. "To live is Christ, to die is gain." In an instant, I went from believing it in my head to believing it in my bone marrow. For as long as it lasted, I couldn't imagine how anyone could ever be afraid of anything. If that is the faith that

TIP #1 FOR
SURVIVING HOSPITALS

Take seriously the words of James 4:2, "You do not have because you do not ask." I have found I was depriving myself of many things I wanted because I didn't ask. The more you ask, the more the staff likes it (usually). It was only on my third hospitalization, when I was feeling terminally grungy, that it occurred to me to ask if the hospital had a shower. It had a beautiful one. When, after three days of not drinking anything, I decided the grapefruit slices were ambrosia and asked if they had more, I got enough to start my own fruit stand. When I decided my pain medication wasn't adequate and asked for something better, I got something that made me sleep like a baby. Don't be a passive patient. It is not only unpleasant; it can also be dangerous.

Jesus had in his Father, no wonder he never understood human fear.

Jesus was there, and while he was there, it was impossible to want anything else. I didn't want to ask, "Why?" If he had the answers, I didn't need to. I didn't ask for any particular outcome. He was going to do the best thing, so why worry?

I know It sounds like a form of insanity. But if it is not, it unmasks the way I usually think as a form of insanity. The two ways of seeing reality are mutually incompatible.

The feeling of his presence lasted about a week. It left a wonderful aftertaste. Now in times of discouragement or fear, I recall the memory. I know him. We spent a week hanging out together. I know what he is like. If I can't feel it at the moment, that doesn't change his nature in the slightest.

With it comes a great sadness and frustration. I have this great glowing thing in my heart, and I can't get it out of my heart and give it to someone else. When I see someone making herself miserable carrying a grudge against God, or feeling lonely and hopeless and abandoned, I want to scream, "It doesn't have to be like that. He wants to give you something much better. Can't you open yourself and receive it?" The looks of suspicion and hostility I get when I make that suggestion make me want to cry.

☘ A Lesson ☘

Coziness

In the theological tradition I come from (liberal Midwestern mainline Protestantism of the 1960s vintage) nobody would ever recommend "coziness" as a positive theological symbol. It was axiomatic back then that the job of a pastor was to "comfort the afflicted and afflict the comfortable." The impact of that from an emotional point of view was to instill a deep suspicion of any kind of comfort. If you were afflicted, it was acceptable to ask for some comfort, but if you ever got really comfortable, you had better watch out, because in some unspecified manner, you needed to be afflicted. Some kind of middle ground where you were a bit comfortable and a bit afflicted was all you could hope for without feeling guilty.

I want to raise an objection.

My first conscious experience of coziness was sitting on the sofa with my father when he read to me from the Childcraft book of poems for early childhood. We would sit together, very close, with a blanket over our laps (unnecessary because the room was always adequately heated), and I would revel in the excessive warmth, the sense of safety, and the incredible silliness of the poetry. Reading poems about "The Little Old Man of the Sea," who saved his boat from sinking by making a hole in the bottom with his knife, "so that all of the water ran out," just added to the pleasure.

I have never lost my connoisseur's appreciation for coziness, especially when I am feeling under the weather. The worse I feel, the more I appreciate it. It seems like a special grace given at times of special need. To be not just warm, but really warm, preferably wrapped in a blanket (preferably electric), and snuggled in it up to your neck still gives a feeling of well-being and safety that I have come to treasure after months of chemotherapy.

And why not? If Jesus insisted that we enter the Kingdom of Heaven like little children, what speaks more clearly of a healthy relationship between a child and a father than that cozy snuggle before bedtime? I remember it as a time of absolute trust, of my littleness and his bigness being a source of security and pleasure — in short, a wonderful symbol of what a healthy relationship with God ought to be.

With so many people I talk to, the main spiritual problem might be diagnosed as a kind of "coziness deficiency." God may be feared, in the wrong sense. God may be respected, and even admired, from a safe distance. But the God who takes such a personal interest in us that he counts each hair on our head, who promises to meet our needs if we will just rearrange our priorities to put him first, a God who can absolutely, no kidding, cross-my-heart-and-hope-to-die be trusted — that God never appears on the radar screen.

I am starting to suspect that when he used the term "faith," Jesus had in mind a relationship with God in which what I am calling "coziness" plays a large part. Faith seems to imply a total lack of fear, a certainty that we are loved, a child's expectation of good things. In fact, I used to feel a little guilty praying flat on my back in my La-Z-Boy. I felt even a little extra guilty when I fell asleep. What could getting comfortable have to do with spirituality?

Now I am starting to think that trusting God enough to get cozy with him may bring the same joy to his heart that my father felt in those blessed evenings on the sofa. Fathers love to be trusted. I think Jesus settled it when he said, "If you, then, who are evil know how to give good gifts to your children, how much more will your Father in heaven...."

⚛ ⚛ ⚛

Given her background she was, and had a right to act like, a princess. Instead, she was a quivering wreck hiding under my sofa.

She was a show quality, pure-blooded Persian cat. Her problem is that when we found her at the animal rescue shelter, she had spent most of her life in a house with three small children and a large German Shepherd. Her life until then had consisted of hiding behind the television set.

Beverly had wanted a longhaired cat for years, and we were very excited. But when we got home and opened the cat carrier, all we saw was a gray streak headed for the sofa.

For the next several weeks, she resisted all attempts to lure her out. When I tried to grab her and force her out, she viciously attacked my hand, ignoring the fact that she had been declawed. It felt like being flogged with Q-Tips. It was actually sort of pathetic.

The only thing we could do was let her hide as long as she needed to. We put the litter pan and food dish next to the sofa and waited.

It took about a month, but one evening we saw her sitting on the rug on the other side of the room staring at us. She seemed to have a lonely look as though she was saying, "Gee, I wish I could get closer."

Something in her ancestry seemed to be telling her that she was made for companionship with people. She wanted it, and she was afraid of it. We knew she had nothing to be afraid of and that we wanted nothing but good for her, but we had no way to convince her. This was a battle she had to fight for herself.

Over the next several weeks, Julie moved closer and closer. Then one fateful day, she jumped into my lap. She just stood there, with a panicky look in her eye, for a few seconds before jumping back down. It wasn't much, but a major barrier had been overcome.

Gradually she took to jumping in my lap more often, and staying longer. Each time I tried to make it as pleasant an experience as I could. Then she started sitting in my lap rather than standing. When she finally started letting me scratch her behind the ears and actually fell asleep, I knew we had arrived.

    ☸ ☸ ☸

God feels about us very much the way I feel about my cat. At the beginning of our relationship with God, almost everyone I know suffers from deep fears of him. I am not sure why this is, but many people have described these fears to me. The worst part is that what are felt as mild anxieties when God is perceived as off at a distance can become outright panic attacks or worse if we feel ourselves getting closer to him.

I remember talking to a woman who had been faithfully involved in the church for many years and had a good deal of theological training who complained that God seemed distant and her prayer life was dry. She was looking for an explanation and vaguely suggesting that God was not keeping up his end of the bargain.

I suggested that we pray together and ask Jesus to show her what the problem was. I laid my hands on her head, as I generally do, and asked Jesus to come close. Almost immediately I felt her stiffen. I asked what was happening and she said, "I actually felt Jesus coming close, and I ran away."

She seemed game for another try. She said, "This time, I will hold on to myself and not let myself run away." We prayed again for a few minutes, and I asked what was happening.

"Jesus came again, and I ran away again."

I asked if she had any idea why she was doing that. "I felt that if I let him get too close, he would see what I am really like and he would hate me."

Seemingly childish words from a very sophisticated woman. That is one way to tell that you are listening to words straight from the heart. She knew intellectually it was ridiculous. In her heart the "ridiculous" fear was an almost insurmountable barrier.

I have known many, many people like this. They can be new to the faith, or old hands, of all levels of intelligence. They can come from abusive home situations, but they can equally well be children of deeply healthy, caring parents. In my experience, people who don't struggle with these anxieties when they start to get serious about their spiritual lives are in the small minority.

We all seem prone to take our past hurts and blame them on God, convincing ourselves that if he hurt us in the past, he will do it again in the future. That is what my cat was doing. When she looked at me, she didn't really see me at all. She saw the three little kids and the German Shepherd and said to herself, "Here we go again."

And just as I felt for my cat, God does not want us to be afraid of him. He wants to love and comfort us, not hurt us.

But God is limited as to how he can reassure us. When I tried to force my attention on my cat by crawling under the sofa and trying to pet her, I only succeeded in making her more terrified. When Jesus came close to my friend, even though he was invited, he provoked the same reaction.

So Jesus comes and sits on the periphery of our life, not close enough to be frightening, but close enough so we somehow sense he is there, close enough to warm our hearts just a bit with his love. When we peek out from under the sofa, he gently pats his lap and says, "You can come here if you want to, and I wish you would."

To me, this is the essence of prayer. Prayer is inching ourselves out from the sofa and shoving ourselves, in spite of our fears, just a little closer to Jesus. It can be a long process, but the only thing that matters is that however slowly we do it, we are getting closer. And as we get closer and find that nothing catastrophic happens and sense his encouraging smile, it becomes even easier to come closer still.

Till one day, we get up the courage to jump in his lap.

I do not apologize if the intimacy of this metaphor seems a little shocking. Jesus was fond of such expressions of intimacy.

> O Jerusalem, Jerusalem . . . , how often I have longed to gather your children together, as a hen gathers her chicks under her wings, but you were not willing!   —Luke 13:34

Look at the longing! Jesus isn't pleading with us to come to him just because he pities us, although he certainly does that. He longs for us! Just the way I feel about my cat, he wants us to overcome our fear and come so close that he can caress and comfort and protect. But he can't force us. It has to be our decision.

I think the best decision I ever made in my priesthood was to commit myself to a regular prayer time. I remember being brash enough to tell my parish vestry, "I hope you understand that every day one hour of work is not going to get done, but I will be praying. You need me to pray more than you need me to do that extra hour of work."

They accepted it, praise God. Over the years they became positively proud of it, and of their willingness to support it. My success at keeping my prayer time wasn't perfect, but I estimate I managed about 85 percent.

Henri Nouwen calls this kind of prayer "dwelling in the healing presence of Jesus." Richard Foster says, "With simplicity of heart we allow ourselves to be gathered up into the arms of the Father and let him sing his love song over us."

Whatever we say about it, it works. I used to struggle with a terrible fear of God, but I have been stroked and scratched behind the ears too many times to take that fear seriously any more. I am intensely happy that I started praying some time ago. I needed to be confident of God's love, given what I was about to go through.

Two

Getting the News

I don't think anyone ever went into surgery with more confidence than I had when I went to the Hudson Valley Hospital Center to have my large intestine removed. I had undergone a very similar operation eight months before and had come through it well. I had had a colonoscopy four months earlier that showed no trace of cancer, or even anything precancerous. The surgery was simply to prevent the possible occurrence of cancer in the future. I remember saying to Beverly something like, "I sure am glad I know what the outcome of this is going to be. If I went in wondering if I had cancer, it would be very hard to take."

How little we know about what is waiting for us just around the corner.

The operation was performed, and I spent two days in the intensive care unit, before being moved to a normal floor. The only surprise was that when I was moved, my wheelchair was taken into a small cubicle where my surgeon was waiting with a rather grim look on her face.

Dr. Meo is a very compassionate person, but when giving someone bad news, she has decided (rightly, I think) that the most compassionate approach is to be as direct as possible.

"Father Simmons, when we removed your colon, I found a two and a quarter centimeter tumor. We will have to wait for the pathology report to be sure, but I am almost certain that it is malignant. One of your lymph nodes was also involved and we removed it too. I was astonished. I just stood there looking at it and not believing what I was seeing."

I was too foggy from the morphine to remember what else she said, except that Beverly had known for two days, and Dr. Meo had asked her not to tell me until I was out of ICU. I had the presence of mind to ask two questions.

"Forgive my asking, but with all the drugs in my system I need to be sure. Is there any possibility that I am dreaming?"

"Father Simmons, I solemnly assure you, you are not dreaming."

"You must love your job."

"This part of it I hate!"

That night I had no thoughts, only feelings. I felt as though I was a plaything in the hands of something horribly evil. I was too dopey to pray, too muddled to think. If I imagine what damnation would feel like, I think it would feel like this.

TIP #2 FOR
SURVIVING HOSPITALS

If you have a regular prayer routine, don't get mad at yourself if you can't maintain it in the hospital. There is just too much going on.

The impossible had happened. My whole future life had been redefined in about four sentences, and I was absolutely helpless to do anything about it.

As my morphine intake went down, my mind was able to bring its own defenses to bear. I simply felt numb. Beverly and I were able to talk about the facts. She shared how difficult it had been knowing this but not being able to share it. There was a real sense of relief for both of us being able to share this burden together. But through all this, my real emotions were, blessedly, out of reach.

From one point of view, I was surprised how little new information I had. I had been told I might die. I always knew that, if not with the same immediacy. I had been told my doctor didn't know when. That told me nothing new either. All that had happened was that my mortality had changed from a vague idea in the back of my mind to the concrete reality it always was. I was simply seeing the reality that had always been there without my usual denial.

> Lord, teach us to number our days,
> that we may apply our hearts to wisdom.
> —Psalm 90:12

That prayer had suddenly been answered. I could only hope the outcome would be wisdom.

Three

Are You Saved, Brother?

"I have cancer."

For several weeks after learning the news, the thought hung in the back of my mind like an ever present dark cloud. I would wake up in the morning and think, "I have cancer." I would think of my family, or my future, or whether it was time to replace our hundred-thousand-mile car, and each time, I would think, "I have cancer."

Lying in bed in the hospital, and later at home, with an eight-inch incision in my belly, gave me a great deal more time to think about it than I might have had otherwise. Knowing almost nothing about what it would be like to have cancer just meant that while my fantasies wouldn't go away, they also wouldn't get me any closer to a realistic idea of my future. They just spun in circles, uselessly but relentlessly.

What would chemotherapy be like? What about having cancer actually kills you? How good is the current state of pain management? Can I keep working?

I had no idea.

TIP #3 FOR
SURVIVING HOSPITALS

If you happen to have nursing training or experience, don't tell anybody. Some nurses will expect you to take responsibility for your own care (ridiculous as that sounds). You are there to be taken care of. Don't let anybody off the hook.

   P.S.: If you happen to be clergy, tell everybody. A hospital room is one of the most productive places imaginable to do ministry.

There was only one fact that seemed solid in the middle of all the uncertainty. I could be dead a great deal sooner than I had thought.

I had taught my congregation for decades that Christians are not afraid of death. That had, of course, been theoretical death, other people's deaths. Now, of course, that had changed, or as they might say on television — "Father Simmons, this death's for you." Real death, potentially within months, no guarantee you can escape it.

Now, all those great-sounding things you have said to other people...how do they play now? You are fixing to be launched into a level of reality far beyond the wildest Star Trek fantasy, a supernatural level where you don't know the rules, where you can control nothing, and where Scripture says spending eternity banished from the presence of God is a possibility. Now, does what you have been saying to others all this time work for you?

Praise God, it does!

Not that I didn't have some hollow feelings in the pit of my stomach thinking about it. Anyone who takes the Bible seriously has to take damnation seriously, however little the church likes to talk about it. Being a religious professional seems to increase the danger rather than lessen it (consider the Pharisees). But as I considered it, I found a number of things very reassuring.

I knew who Jesus was. I had talked to him and felt his presence a number of times. The time in the emergency room before my first surgery should answer that

question all by itself. I had been in the presence of
Love. I had been touched by the divine gentleness. I
had felt myself an element in the divine joy. What more
reassurance could anyone want?

I am convinced Jesus' heart aches for every person to
be with him in heaven. The cross shows he is willing
to pay the highest price to make the road as easy as
possible for us.

So I applied this to myself— "Jesus wants to give it.
I want to receive it. It's a done deal."

It worked. It made spiritual sense and psychologi-
cal sense. I could relax — and I did. That was four
months ago, and I don't think I have had a twinge of
fear of death since. Beverly and I talk about it openly.
Sometimes I think we even shock our friends. If the
time comes, we will plan my funeral together, and in
a strange sense, I am even looking forward to it.

The one thing I won't do is be afraid of it. How
can going home to your best friend be the least bit
frightening?

Four

Interrogating the Doctor

I have just entrusted my life to a man who, if he were a Christian, I would unhesitatingly describe as a saint. Since he isn't, and his tradition doesn't use the word, I don't have a label for him. I just wish God would send a hundred thousand more just like him.

I am attracted primarily to his humanness. He is a delightful mix of scientist and bohemian. He can preside over a hi-tech medical office and leave you in no doubt that he has read all the most recent research, and then shamble out of the office in a leather jacket and baseball cap as though defiantly rejoicing in his own dumpiness. If he wants to look like a grocery packer in a supermarket, nobody can stop him. He is free to be exactly who he is. In his presence, I feel that I can be exactly who I am.

In a practice where he sees as many as a hundred seriously sick people a day, he has the uncanny ability to sympathize deeply with those who are suffering, and then almost instantly rejoice with someone who is receiving good news. He seems to float over it all, supported by his own serenity, while never being the least bit distant. However long it takes, I am determined to discover his secret.

Still, I didn't accept him as my oncologist without making him sweat for it.

When my wife and I first met him, it was clear he had thoroughly studied my medical history. He did not downplay the difficulties we faced. "Metastatic colon cancer is a tough nut. Still, I have a good number of patients who came in sicker than you are who are going strong five years later. We have a lot of treatment options for colon cancer, so we should be able to find something that will do a good job for you."

The perfect balance — positive and optimistic, while avoiding making promises he can't keep or whitewashing the difficulties. I started to feel I had come to the right place.

I felt this was the time to define our relationship, and I wanted it to be a relationship of equals. I had come with a good many questions, and I started asking them. What about a second opinion? Should I consider a clinical trial? Would the chemo leave me able to work? Since he knew I was going to do independent reading, were there any books I should focus on, or books I should avoid?

For each question I received a clear answer, with patient explanations of anything I didn't understand. He seemed to have all the time in the world.

TIP #4 FOR
SURVIVING HOSPITALS

If you are not comfortable with a drug or course of treatment,

demand an explanation, and if you are not satisfied, refuse

it. You have lived in your body more than they have, and if

something just doesn't feel right, say so.

Finally the blockbuster. I still don't know where I got the nerve to ask this question, but it turned out to be the deal-clincher. "I want you to know that I consider myself to be my own primary care manager, and my doctors work for me. Can you handle that?"

I had expected a variety of reactions, but not the one I got. He leaned back in his chair with a dreamy look in his eye that looked like, and was, a moment of real pleasure. "That . . . is exactly the kind of patient I want."

The bond was cemented. From that moment on, I knew he would be loyal to me, and I was determined to be loyal to him. It was more than a doctor-patient relationship; it was a friendship, and it has continued to grow ever since.

I can't overstate what a comfort it is to have a competent, compassionate, and humble doctor when you are facing as formidable an enemy as cancer. I know there are cancer patients who sign on with the first doctor they meet, whether he is a heartless mechanic, a tyrant, or a nincompoop. I think that is tragically irresponsible. There are wonderful doctors out there. I think I deserve one. I think you do too.

On his desk, in the middle of a massive collection of signed baseballs and vacation pictures, my doctor has a plaque with this prayer:

> Lord, as I treat my patients
>   Help me to be wise;
> Let me see their problems
>   Through your discerning eyes.
> Guide me, Lord, and use me
>   In everything I do,
> For You're the Great Physician,
>   And I long to be like you.
>   — Robin Fogle

He doesn't know how close he is.

Five

The First Chemo Treatment

My introduction to chemotherapy was very impressive. I was given a computer-driven pump that administers state-of-the-art medication very gradually through a "life port" in my chest and directly into the superior vena cava. I am a tech freak anyway, and I found this all very satisfying and reassuring. It fit seamlessly into my lifestyle, occupying a spot on my belt next to my cell phone, and just over the pocket where I keep my Palm Pilot. In the mornings I left my house feeling almost at one with the crew of the Starship Enterprise. With all of this technology, all things have to be possible.

Unfortunately, I now know with the benefit of hind-sight that, in my case, all this glitzy technology was

absolutely useless. Two and a half months after starting therapy, Dr. F. informed us with a doleful look
on his face that the tumors had grown two and a
half times bigger than they were at the last scan. The
blood markers were also going haywire at an alarming
rate. We were obviously dealing with an extremely fast-
growing, aggressive cancer, and the medication wasn't
touching it.

The down side of being a tech freak is that I could
do the math. If the tumor doubles approximately every
two months, how long would it take before it was big
enough to fill my garage? I never did the calculations,
but I knew it wouldn't take long.

Dr. F. is a very honest man, but he knows when not to
gratuitously pile gloomy facts one on top of the other.
He could have said that the tumors were starting to
seriously affect my liver function, and, at this rate, it
would be only a short time before my eyes turned a
bright yellow. He could have said — but didn't until
several months later — that I was "racing downhill with
all the brakes off."

What he did say was, "I am the eternal optimist,
but . . . "

Dr. F. explained that he had already switched me to
the other standard colon cancer treatment, based on
CPT-11, saying, "We need to find something to shrink
these things, and fast!" When I asked about how many

people are helped by CPT-11, he said it was about 50 percent.

Judging from the CAT scan results and the increased feelings of pressure in my abdomen, I knew that Dr. F. wouldn't have time to try very many different treatments. If the CPT-11 didn't work, I was in big trouble. And its chances of working were the same as the flip of a coin. Heads I live, at least for a while. Tails I die.

⚜ ⚜ ⚜

The outer shell of technology — the flashing liquid crystal screens, the reassuring click as the medication was delivered — had lulled me into an unquestioning assumption that it was all going to work. For something so impressive to be a total failure seemed obscene, but there it was.

Oncology is, basically, the science of throwing mud at a wall and seeing what sticks. It cannot predict what, if any, course of treatment will help a particular patient. It can only try to produce stickier mud.

The thought that came next shouldn't have been a shock, but it was. "There are problems out there that we can't fix." I suppose that on an emotional level I had assumed that some new invention, some new drug, some more accurate research data, or some new governmental policy would either solve any serious problem I faced or at least reduce it to something I could live with. This was pretty much the way my life had been up until then.

It wasn't the way my life was going to be in the future. I thought, "This thing in you may be invincible. It might just seize control of your insides like Godzilla, contemptuous of all attempts to stop it. It might rupture vital organs, shut down your liver, inflict severe pain when and where it feels like it, like a cat playing with a mouse, and the best medical people in the world can only look on sympathetically but helplessly." This could be a problem with no solution.

My sense of shock and betrayal should have told me that what I thought I believed was not what I actually believed. I thought I believed something like:

> Unless the LORD builds the house,
>   its builders labor in vain.
> Unless the LORD watches over the city,
>   the watchmen stand guard in vain.
> —Psalm 127:1

If asked, I would have told you that my life was completely dependent on God and that I knew it and approved of it. To actually experience the cold fact that there really is nothing else to depend on and discover that I didn't like it one bit knocked me out of my complacency. Like most Americans, when I have a problem, I have a list of things I depend on before I depend on God (doctors, bankers, lawyers, credit cards). I like to

TIP #5 FOR
SURVIVING HOSPITALS

*If you happen to be the sort of Christian who knows how to re-
spect someone else's right to say no (not all do), don't hesitate
to offer to pray for people. People want prayer at a time like this.
I worked with a volunteer ambulance company for seven years
and never saw anyone reject a prayer in the back of an ambulance, or even seem offended at the offer (and I think I can read
people's emotions fairly accurately). Somehow people know
you have something they need. Forget this nonsense about our
"secular society." That façade is only about a micron deep. Inter-
estingly, I had a roommate who was told he could go home if he
was able to urinate. He wasn't, and he was getting frustrated. I
offered to pray for him, and he sprang a leak in ten minutes. He
went home with great rejoicing.*

solve my own problems with my own resources and tip my hat to God afterward. It is a bad habit that has been undermining my faith for years.

Every so often I have been privileged to meet someone who really depended on God first, and it has always been a shock. I am thinking particularly of a funny little guy who is involved in one of the prominent Christian ministries in Kenya. He is a good friend of parishioners in my former parish. Having lunch with him is like being hauled off into the time of the Bible. In an unvarying tone of lighthearted enthusiasm, he tells nonstop stories of healings, miracles, whole villages abandoning animism for Christianity. At one point when we were having lunch, I couldn't stand any more and stopped him dead in his tracks. He was particularly involved in his story:

> There was a village that was completely dominated by a witch. Everyone was terrified of her. One night our team went there, and we sent one man into the village while the rest of us stayed in the bushes and prayed. He confronted the witch, and when she tried to put a curse on him, he....

I lost it. "Hold it, John!"

He looked at me, surprised but curious as I asked what was half a question and half an ashamed confession. "Can you tell me why all of these things are happening in Kenya, but we don't see them here?"

I had expected painful criticism. What I got were words of compassionate wisdom that I will always be grateful for:

> Jeff, Kenya was not always like this. There are two reasons for the change. First, there are many people who have prayed passionately for renewal in that part of Africa for over thirty years. Many of them have died without seeing the results of their prayers, but the spiritual power that has been poured out on our country is directly due to their faithfulness. Second, we are such a poor people that when we get into trouble we know we have no place to turn but to God.

John recounted a night when he was a teenager when the food in the house ran out. His father had to make a decision. He told the youngest children in the family, "You will eat tonight." He told his older children, "You will pray tonight." It was a horribly painful experience for him.

The older children prayed, the intensity of their prayers aided by the emptiness of their stomachs. About midnight, an uncle from a neighboring village walked into their house with several bags of groceries, saying, "I was praying, and I think I was told that you needed this."

John had had some difficult lessons on his way to learning to trust God, but he had learned his lesson well. It is almost impossible to imagine him being afraid of anything. When life sends new experiences, he throws himself into the middle of them, confident that he can't get himself into any trouble that God can't get him out of.

What is the difference between John and me? John is "poor in spirit," or as he would say it, "When we get into trouble, we know we have no place to turn but to God" (see Matthew 5:3). I particularly like the Bible translations that say, "Blessed are those who know their need of God." John has been in need of God so many times, and (here is where he differs from so many people) so joyfully open to God's intervention, and so instantly obedient when he senses what God wants him to do, that his need of God has become a source of power.

I am not particularly "poor in spirit," but one of the benefits of having cancer is that it is very likely to make me more so. There are fewer and fewer places I can turn for help, medically, financially, or in many other ways. I may come to the point where I can choose hopelessness or a much more radical rejoicing in my poverty of spirit.

I want to become like John, and, in this, the cancer is a real ally.

Six

Misery Is Optional

When Julie, my cat, climbs into my lap, she likes to move her paws up and down like she was kneading bread. This is common, of course, and I have heard people speculate that this is how kittens let the mother cat know that they want her to let down her milk.

Julie, however has a special place for this — right on my ostomy bag.* Having made delicious squishy noises, she often lies down with her head right on the

---

*For the uninitiated, an ostomy is a surgical procedure where either the small or large intestine is cut, and the cut portion inserted through a hole in the abdominal wall so that it projects outside. It looks like nothing so much as a large cherry Life Saver stuck to one's abdomen. The contents of the intestine then drain into a special plastic bag held in place by a patch of adhesive. Sometimes the ostomy is temporary and the sections of the intestine will be rejoined in another operation. In my case, it is permanent. I will never see another bedpan, which is not a bad thing.

bag. Again, I am very grateful that someone had her declawed.

Beverly has remarked on my exemplary hospitality. Not only do I offer a warm lap, but how many laps are equipped with a water bed?

Ostomies are one of the pieces of genuinely good news in this whole saga. Unless a person is allergic to the materials, an ostomy is easy to maintain, comfortable, and in the opinion of many inflammatory bowel disease sufferers, brings a great improvement in quality of life.

When I was in my thirty-year struggle with ulcerative colitis, I lived in fear of emergencies. Most colitis patients go through life with a constantly updated estimate of how many old ladies we will have to knock over in a mad rush to the nearest bathroom. We also are constantly aware of the limitations of our diet — eating a strawberry had become as inconceivable to me as voluntarily spooning broken glass into my mouth.

Now the emergencies are a thing of the past. So is my diet. I know I will live as far as summer, because the promise of one's first fresh strawberry shortcake in thirty years should be enough to keep anyone alive!

And I have met one of the goofiest groups of people in the world, those who write to the United Ostomy Association bulletin board. Writers to the bulletin board tend to fall into two categories. There are those who are facing an operation in which an ostomy is a possibility or a certainty, and they are scared and full of anxious questions. Then there are those who have had the surgery, most of whom are evangelically enthusiastic about it. Many view it as an actual improvement over the traditional way humans do their business.

TIP #6 FOR
SURVIVING HOSPITALS

As my dad used to say about being drafted into the army, "You are going to go for two years, no matter what. I have known guys who made themselves miserable the whole time. I have known others who just decided they were going to be happy and went about doing it. Happiness is not something that just happens to you. You have to decide you want it."

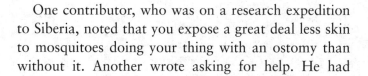

One contributor, who was on a research expedition to Siberia, noted that you expose a great deal less skin to mosquitoes doing your thing with an ostomy than without it. Another wrote asking for help. He had successfully played nearly every known sport without trouble with his ostomy. His one unsolvable problem was surfing. Nothing he had tried would keep the bag on when he took a really large wave, and he wanted to know if anyone had any suggestions.

One wag observed that if God had had plastic at the creation, he would have done the nice thing and given everyone an ostomy.

And yet the literature I was given in the hospital after my operation says that some people never get past the shock of having an ostomy. They let their depression over their condition dominate their lives and just withdraw from the world.

I guess there are always two ways of looking at everything. What do they say in AA? "Pain is unavoidable. Misery is optional."

Guess that about says it all.

Seven

The Martyrdom of Monotony

Let's see . . . I've been up for two hours now. I have irrigated my nasal passages thoroughly to eliminate the blood clots that form because of the chemo. I have drunk a good deal of water and fruit juice to replace fluid lost during the night (my stomach rebels at the thought of drinking more than eight ounces of water each of the five or so times my dry mouth wakes me up at night). I have checked my ostomy wafer to make sure there won't be any embarrassing accidents (a little bit of engineering background is helpful here). I fixed the highest calorie breakfast I thought I could tolerate, since my bathroom scale told me after last week's hospitalization that I weighed only 120 pounds. I have downed a handful of pills with names so long and intimidating that I have stopped even trying to learn them. Now I am ready to start the day.

Other people's bodies just get up and function. Mine needs to have every detail supervised.

TIP #7 FOR
SURVIVING HOSPITALS

Bring your computer, if you are comfortable with the security

of the hospital, or if you have someone to take it home at

night. E-mail is a good cure for loneliness and isolation. You

can usually disconnect the phone line and plug it right into the

computer. My hospital even has data ports on its telephones!

None of this is particularly painful. No one job by itself is all that difficult or time consuming. Nothing here to inspire comments at a eulogy about "fighting a courageous battle against cancer." Just dumb, and in some cases humiliating, jobs that have to be done again and again, whether your body feels good or on the point of exhaustion.

Gradually it takes its toll. I find myself getting grumpy or feeling guilty about the things Beverly and I would like to do together but can't because I am not up to it. I start comparing myself to other people, or to what I could do a year ago, and start to feel like a freak.

Here, I think, is the real battle. Classic Christianity insists that in the supernatural realm I have both friends and enemies and that I have to take both seriously. My friends are treating my medical condition as a wonderful opportunity for growth. My enemies, the devil and company, see it as an opportunity for my destruction.

While it would get me laughed out of most seminaries in the country, I refuse to apologize for talking about the devil. When people ask me, "Do you still believe in that old superstitious nonsense?" I like to answer, "Whether I believe it or not isn't all that important, but I know for certain my Lord believed it, and I am very hesitant to pick a fight with him."

I don't find belief in supernatural evil upsetting. Quite the contrary, I find it clarifies some issues in a way that is comforting. I am convinced, along with virtually every Christian I know who thinks this way, that Satan had his fangs pulled on Good Friday, and that, in Christ, I am much more powerful than he is, provided I use the power I have been given consistently and intelligently.

I also know, as every cancer patient knows, that there is real devilment going on in my life. I can't see my cancer as anything but evil, and I see no scriptural reason to even try. To see an evil cancer coming from an evil source strikes me as intellectually and emotionally satisfying. What would be intolerable is to believe that God himself was inflicting this on me, which is a conclusion that Christians who reject the idea of the devil have a very hard time avoiding. Knowing you have been clobbered by an enemy is a great deal happier thought than thinking your friends did it to you.

The same is true of the daily irritations and temptations I am facing. Here I find the modern psychology I studied in seminary, based heavily on Freud and Jung, is not particularly helpful. One of the main ideas seems to be that all the thoughts going around in my head are my thoughts — they were generated by my mind, either the conscious or the unconscious. The healthy thing to do with them, then, is to be aware of them, understand them, and "make friends" with them as I develop a more whole personality. In this view, if I find my head full of destructive thoughts, there doesn't seem much I can do about it.

I am coming to prefer the viewpoint of the first Christian monastics, the Desert Fathers and Mothers of fourth- and fifth-century Egypt. In their view, some of our thoughts do not originate with us at all, but are, in a sense, inserted in our minds from outside, often with hostile intent. They sap our courage, inflame our fears, stir up our anger and self-pity, and deplete a lot of emotional energy at times when we need all the energy we have.

The solution, according to the desert monastics, is to aggressively take control of the thoughts in our heads, or as Ignatius Loyola says:

> To understand to some extent the different movements produced in the soul and to recognize those that are good to admit them, and those that are bad, to reject them.
> — Ignatius Loyola, *Spiritual Exercises*, §313

It is a strange idea to most people that our minds contain bad thoughts that should simply be tossed out like last week's leftover fish, but many of the spiritual masters took it for granted. I think cancer patients are in a better position to understand this than most. Our minds fill up with garbage ideas very fast. A few of the more common ones are:

- I am a freak.
- It is somehow my fault that I have cancer.
- Other people are being seriously inconvenienced by my cancer, and I should feel guilty for it.
- My disease is meaningless.
- This proves God is unfair, and life is a bad joke.
- I shouldn't need to take all these pills, go for all these treatments, etc.

These thoughts can swirl around in our minds (or my mind at least) like flies over garbage cans, and they can keep it up indefinitely. They can undermine our peace and happiness, make us withdrawn and resentful, alienate the very people we need to look to for help, and send our self-pity through the roof. The best way to deal with them is to recognize them, throw them out of our minds, and deliberately focus on the truth. The truth is:

- I am not a freak. I am a person with dignity like everybody else. A very large number of wonderful people get cancer. I am part of a large group.

- I did not choose to get cancer. It just happened, and there is no reason to feel guilty about it.

- It is not bad to need help at times like this. If it is really "better to give than to receive," I am a source of blessing for a good many people.

- Somehow in the economy of God, my disease was not unexpected or meaningless. It is preparing for me an "eternal weight of glory."

- God is not unfair and has not lost control.

- I do need all these pills and treatments, and I have no reason to feel bad about that either.

Many people call this "self talk," and it can be a very powerful force for emotional health, if it is used with determination and consistency. One of the main reasons we do not use it consistently is that the destructive ideas often seem so unimportant that we don't feel the need to defend ourselves. Therein lies the danger.

I think it was C. S. Lewis who pointed out that most of Satan's attacks are banal and undramatic. There is a reason for that. If Satan only sent major attacks, like burning your house down, you would probably respond by mobilizing your defenses, your faith, courage, obedience to God, etc. For Satan, the best attack is just intense enough to make us irritable, self-centered, and discouraged without being so intense that we see what is happening and mobilize our defenses. Hence the value to us of monotony.

It's the tired monotony of waking up to the same list of pills, treatments, nasal sprays, and thinning hair that makes our battle so difficult. But this is also the battleground on which souls are won or lost.

St. Anthony of Egypt once wanted to serve God by being martyred, but when Constantine's legalization of Christianity made that impossible, he returned to his cell, where he became a "daily martyr to his conscience" (Aelred Squire, *Asking the Fathers*). As Christians and cancer patients, I think we are called to the daily martyrdom of monotony. But the victory will be no less glorious because of the drabness of the battlefield.

Eight

The Doctor Who Almost Killed Me

My surgeon is more than happy to lay down the law when she thinks it is necessary.

"Father Simmons, you are a young man, and you need to make sure that you are getting the most up-to-date treatment for your condition. In your case, it is mandatory to get a second opinion from someone in a top-notch research hospital."

I chose a hospital where a friend of mine was already receiving treatment. She is a nurse herself, and during her chemo treatments, she had been watching the various doctors. She was also strong in her opinions. "The doctor you want to talk to is Dr. X."

So armed with my various documents, I went. The doctor seemed like a competent, businesslike man, although perhaps a little aloof. He went over my history in detail and suggested that he would personally use a slightly different mix of drugs, but that there was nothing wrong with what my oncologist was doing. Then he started talking about the disease in general.

"You know that chemotherapy is not a cure. It is something we do to try to buy our patients a little bit of time before the end."

TIP #8 FOR
SURVIVING HOSPITALS

Keep track of the names of star performers among the medical staff. You will probably be given a chance to put in a good word for outstanding nurses and aides, and they will appreciate it.

My eyes bored two neat, half-inch holes in his skull, trying to see into his brain. "A little bit of time?"

He stared back at me. He was not a man to back down. "Yes, a little bit of time."

"In that case, what is the point of doing chemo-therapy at all?"

He put his head in his hands. "That . . . is a very good question."

He invited me to do my own research, but added a warning. "If you read the American Cancer Society material, just be aware that they are likely to be a good deal too optimistic. They want to make it look like we are making progress."

Criminals just condemned to the gallows don't get the privilege of driving home after leaving the court-room, but if they did, they would have almost the same experience I did. I called my wife from my cell phone in a rest area parking lot off the interstate and told her that an expert had just assured me I was going to die. No options, no place to turn, no hope.

Dr. X submitted my case to a "tumor board" to get the opinion of his colleagues and called me later that day. "I have been talking to an expert in colo-rectal cancers. He agrees that colon cancer that is caused by ulcerative colitis doesn't usually respond to chemotherapy."

Dr. X's words said "doesn't usually"; his tone of voice said, "A cold day in hell when. . . . "

"It is almost a whole different kind of biology," Dr. X continued. "There is no reason to change anything I told you last time." His voice sounded almost triumphant.

Great! "A whole different kind of biology." Now I am not just fighting ordinary cancer, I am being invaded by aliens! I made a promise to myself that next time I had a chance to look at my X-rays and CAT scans, I would look carefully for evidence of flying saucers.

The best way to appreciate the value of hope is to have it taken away from you. My oncologist back home was an excellent doctor, but my doom had just been pronounced by someone from the major leagues, a noted expert with a long list of research monographs on his resume. Many hamsters had died at his hands. He had to know what he was talking about, didn't he?

What is life without hope? Fighting is futile. Courage is a waste of time. You are nothing but a helpless victim, unable to do anything to influence the inevitable outcome. Before, you were a fighter, a participant, a factor in the equation to be reckoned with. It was a war, and a war lost but well fought carries a certain dignity. Now, you are just a shell containing a relentless pathological process. The whole thing has all the dignity of a worm being smashed under a car tire.

I could feel the energy draining out of my body. I knew I was headed for a depression. It was time to talk to my oncologist, fast.

I tried to lay out to him the facts as objectively as I could, but then I lost it. "As far as I can tell, he is saying the only option I have is to make sure my life insurance is paid up and put a gun to my head."

My doctor just sat open-mouthed and bug-eyed for a moment. "Is this guy trying to kill you?! Don't return his phone calls! Don't answer his mail! Forget he ever said anything!"

I could feel a small spark of light igniting someplace in my mind, a small luminous circle gingerly challenging the darkness. I pressed my advantage. "Have you ever known colon cancer patients with a history of ulcerative colitis to respond to chemotherapy?"

Eliot put all the emphasis he could into his answer. I could imagine his secretaries down the hall spilling their coffee just from the force of it: "YES!"

The light grew brighter. I could feel energy flowing back into my muscles.

"They don't all respond to chemo, but a good many of them do."

It didn't take much to put me back on track emotionally. I didn't need a promise of a cure. I needed hope. I needed a sense that there was a reason to fight back, that there was something I could do, that it made sense to give it my best shot. Anything to lift the soul-killing feeling of total helplessness. Was Dr. X trying to kill me? No. If I had gone into treatment with him, might his attitude have succeeded in killing me? You bet. I wonder how many patients have died from the emotional damage done by doctors like him. I was administered a big dose of toxic pessimism by an expert, and I appreciate its power. I will never allow myself to be treated by someone like that again. Period!

A Lesson

The Extraordinariness
of Prayer

One of the best ways for a lay person to alienate a new priest is to imply that after an expensive theological education and a valid Episcopal ordination, he is still not a real priest until he goes to a certain conference (conveniently coming up the next week) and "gets the spirit."

I am still not sure why I ended up going. It was certainly not because I wanted to be there.

The year was 1979. It turned out to be a large conference of perhaps five hundred people. I came away with three vivid impressions. First, I felt the singing was interminable. Second, I found the talks far better and more convincing than I had expected. Third, I remember a (suspiciously) powerful determination that I was not going to let anybody at the conference pray for me. Had I known what I know now, I would have seen the intensity of my negative emotions as a dead giveaway that something powerful was getting ready to happen.

As I remember, I got through most of the conference dodging offers of prayer and making the people from my parish who had invited me increasingly irritated. At noon on Saturday, when we stopped for an hour-and-a-half lunch break, my only thought was "I have to get out of here." Even a large church, if it is hosting five hundred people, offers few opportunities for solitude. There was, however, a small patch of grass behind the church with a weeping-willow-like tree that couldn't have been more than six feet tall. The advantage was that the foliage reached all the way to the ground. It offered what I needed most — P-R-I-V-A-C-Y.

Sitting with my back against the trunk, I tried to sort out my feelings. I felt trapped (someone else had driven and I didn't have a car). I felt pressured and manipulated. I felt that my emotions were making me act uncomfortably like a little kid. But as the sunlight sparkling through the cool green leaves started to calm me, I became aware that I felt curious and a little ashamed of myself for not being more adventurous.

The theme of the conference, boiled down to the essentials, was nothing more than, "God wants to have a closer and more productive relationship with you, if you will just open yourself to receive it." I couldn't argue with that. To be honest, my real problem was that I was in a battle of wills with two obnoxious parishioners and didn't want to give them the satisfaction of thinking they had won.

Even in my sullen mood at the time I had to admit that wasn't good enough, so I sat under that tree for an hour and a half praying the hardest I had ever prayed in my life, "Dear God, if you have something for me that I don't have, I'll take it here!"

Several decades later, I still look back at that time of prayer with gratitude. I was not aware, when I emerged from under the tree, that anything had changed. It was not an emotional experience at all. The changes happened gradually over the next six months.

Prayer became a hunger, and the sense of God's presence far more intense. The amount of money I spent on Christian books increased dramatically. The biggest change, however, was what happened when I read the Bible. Passages I had read fifty times took on a vividness and urgency that were almost disorienting. I think my wife got a little tired of my charging into the kitchen while she was cooking dinner waving a Bible and yelling, "Now I know what this passage means! Why didn't I ever see it before?"

All I had said was, "God, if you have something for me that I don't have, I'll take it." This is a prayer for everybody. I didn't have to join any faction in the church in order to pray it. It can't, like some prayers I have heard, be used by one group to gain political advantage over another group. It does not imply that anyone else is inadequate or defective. It simply says, as I think Christians should always say, that God always has more for me, and that I am standing before him with empty, receptive hands.

But how different this is from the way I usually pray. Rather than praying with expectancy and receptiveness, my prayers (and those of most of the people I know) usually assume that God is not going to change much, and that we don't really want him to. In fact, I find in spiritual direction that when people are encouraged to pray, really believing that God is going to make a major change in their lives, many find it almost unbearably threatening.

I went back once to see if I could visit my tree. It had been removed to make room for a bigger parking lot. I felt as though a holy shrine had been desecrated. But, then, nobody else had any reason to think so except me.

"God, if you have something for me that I don't have, I'll take it." You could almost see the whole spiritual life as summed up in that prayer. For me it has led to a peace and confidence and intimacy that I wouldn't give up for anything.

The Ordinariness
of Prayer

My wife and I have said Morning Prayer out of the Episcopal Prayer Book about 85 percent of the time for thirty-two years. Much of the time it has not left me particularly excited, but it is for us the church's prayer, a good way to work systematically through the Scriptures, and a way of developing habits of prayerfulness. Otherwise, if you were to ask me, I would have said there are other kinds of prayer that put me in touch with God far more powerfully. I am a "let me sit under a tree for an hour and be with Jesus" kind of guy.

Well, I can't sit under a tree with Jesus in the hospital. Many times the medications fog my mind to the point I can hardly pray spontaneously at all. However, I can work my way through the prayers in the Prayer Book, and I can't overstate what a comfort that is. Brain or no brain, tree or no tree, I can pray, and I am praying with a very large number of people. Tomorrow is Sunday, and Beverly can't be with me, but I can say Morning

Prayer alone and know that I am praying side by side with a vast multitude on both sides of the grave.

In the Episcopal Church we like to refer to this as the "objectivity of prayer." That means that if I feel warm and fuzzy during my prayer time, it's wonderful, but when I feel nothing, that is wonderful too. I don't have to feel that I am being successful in prayer. Any honest attempt at prayer is valuable to me and acceptable to God. The author of *The Cloud of Unknowing* says it better than I can.

> You will seem to know nothing and to feel nothing except a naked intent toward God in the depths of your being. Try as you might, this darkness and this cloud will remain between you and your God. You will feel frustrated, for your mind will be unable to grasp him and your heart will not relish the delight of his love. But learn to be at home in this darkness.

I have heard pastors say that if you don't feel in touch with Jesus, then you have lost contact with Jesus, pure and simple. I can't imagine a more cruel or destructive thing to say, especially to severely ill patients. How many have gone to their deaths thinking they had fallen from grace simply because they couldn't feel his presence! It is a terrible form of abuse of people least able to defend themselves. None of the masters of Christian spirituality talked like that. After all, Jesus did not die on the cross saying "My God, your presence really feels good." He said, "My God, why have you forsaken me?"

The best attitude we can have is to be grateful when we sense his presence, and equally grateful when we don't, trusting that he meant it when he said, "All that the Father gives me will come to me, and whoever comes to me I will never drive away" (John 6:37). You will have to work hard to find any loopholes or escape clauses in that promise!

But, again, the comfort of "objective prayer" is difficult to experience if we start only after a heavy diagnosis. We need to start now, as soon as we can. Relationships like this mature only gradually.

Nine

Climbing Up on the Altar

I have always said that what bothers me most about having cancer is not the fear of dying. It is the fear of leaving Beverly a widow. Coming from a very hearty breed, she could live, like her mother, to age ninety-six, which would mean forty years of getting along without me.

We are very, flamboyantly, unapologetically married. A friend once commented, "There are so many couples who stay married only because they can't get their act together enough to get divorced. Why did this cancer have to happen to the most happily married couple I know?"

In the early days after the diagnosis, the question gnawed at both of us. We would snuggle in bed together, and both of us would silently ask, "How much longer will we be doing this?" I would imagine Beverly buying a house without me, eating her meals without me, getting sick in her turn without me to offer her the same care she was offering me. I knew she was asking the same questions, and it broke my heart.

TIP #9 FOR
SURVIVING HOSPITALS

Take a good pair of eyeshades – the kind you see arrogant movie stars wearing in 1930s films. You can get them in any decent drug store. Most hospital televisions are wall-mounted in a way that floods the whole room with light, and even if you have your eyes closed, it can be very irritating. Fight the urge to be embarrassed.

One Tuesday night, Beverly was praying for me and my healing. We had developed a tradition. I would lie in my recliner, and she would sit next to me with her hand on my abdomen and pray. This particular night she started to cry. I will never forget looking up at her tear-stained face and hearing her say, "I don't want to lose you. I don't want to lose you."

We put our arms around each other and wept for the sheer helplessness of it. The one thing she wanted, and the one thing I wanted to give her more than anything, was not mine to give. I could feel myself slipping away from her, and there wasn't a blessed thing I could do about it — not a blessed thing anybody could do about it.

It was one of the bleakest moments of my life, and it was going to get worse.

That night, Beverly went alone to a community chorus rehearsal. Of course, it had to be that night that she blew a tire on a lonely road on the way home. Luckily someone else from the choir came along and helped change it, but when she got back home, she was half frozen, shivering, and obviously thinking, "Is this what life is going to be like from now on?"

We could feel life spiraling out of control.

The next day, I had planned to go to a healing center called the Oratory of the Little Way in Gaylordsville, Connecticut, where my friend Nigel Mumford was director. They offer a time of "soaking prayer," when sick people just pray quietly for two full hours in a chapel with some intercessors praying for them. Pillows and blankets are provided for those who want to pray lying on the floor. It is a very peaceful and powerful time.

Beverly drove me there, since I was obviously too weak to drive myself. As the car approached the oratory, all her body language said she did not want to be there. She was tense, depressed, and obviously felt she didn't belong.

As I said before, such obvious anxiety is usually a sign that something good is about to happen.

We prayed, gently and quietly, for the full two hours. People prayed for Beverly as well as for me.

During that two hours, it was as if a dark cloud of insanity lifted, and we both saw clearly what we had to do. We both knew we had to relive the story of Abraham's sacrifice of Isaac.

    ☩ ☩ ☩

It is amazing how some of my least favorite Bible passages can turn into beloved friends once I have experienced the same thing and come to understand what is actually being said. The story of God telling Abraham to sacrifice Isaac is a particularly good example.

In the story, God tells Abraham to take his son to the top of Mt. Moriah and kill him. (If this story is new to you, don't turn off quite yet, even though I know it is tempting.) This is the son that Abraham has waited for for twenty-five years since the first time God promised a son to him. Isaac is his only heir. All of Abraham's hopes for happiness are riding on Isaac.

God gives no explanations. He just says, "Do it." Abraham does it, right up to the point of almost plunging the knife into Isaac's heart. As soon as it is absolutely clear that Abraham is determined to obey God no matter what, God stops him and sends the two of them home together. I imagine they must have had a memorable conversation on the road back!

After the session of soaking prayer, and already feeling a great deal more light-hearted than two hours before, Bev and I, with Nigel's help, talked over what had happened and what we were going to do about it. We very deliberately took the story of Abraham's sacrifice and made it our story.

We both admitted to ourselves and each other that, while we had considered ourselves Christians and had thought we were acting like Christians, our emotional reactions had been identical to those of any pagan. We had surrendered to feelings of fear, hopelessness, and total abandonment. In the process, we had been making certain assumptions, and those assumptions had the power to kill us. Hell was opening its mouth, and in a perverse, unconscious way, we were cooperating.

We knew we were going to the top of Mt. Moriah. We had no choice in that. We knew there could be a real death on that altar. But we were free to decide who we believed was calling us up that mountain, what his reasons were, and what kind of response to make.

We decided to believe the God of Abraham was calling us up the mountain. A loving God, who knows exactly what he is doing, and ultimately wills abundant blessing, but who, according to the old hymn, "moves in a mysterious way, his wonders to perform."

That is not the God we had believed in two hours before. Then, just like any pagan, we were reacting as though we were absolutely alone with a meaningless, overwhelming problem on our hands, and no one to help us. We had been acting as though there would be no God to help in the future either, and if Beverly found herself alone, there would be no place to turn for protection from forces far more powerful than her.

Now we decided on a total belief transplant. Our God had promised his presence, his protection, and his love. But like the God of Mt. Moriah, he was a wild, mysterious God. He had not promised that our life would turn out the way we wanted, and as God, he had no obligation to obey our instructions. He was not our house servant; he was our Lord, and free to do whatever he saw fit. But he had promised that he was absolutely aware of our needs (Matthew 6:22), that his agenda was for us to have life and have it abundantly (John 10:10), and that our troubles now were preparing for the future an experience of God's glory that would make our sufferings look trivial in retrospect (2 Corinthians 4:17).

We had to decide if it was true or it wasn't. If it wasn't true, our despair from this morning was realistic, and we could never hope for anything else. If it was true, then we were headed (by the same train or different trains, but still on the same track) for a glorious future, and if we were separated, Bev would always have a trusty friend at her shoulder to comfort and protect her, and we were both safe and had nothing to worry about.

We didn't waste much time making that choice. We both committed ourselves to believing, either with our emotions when that was possible, or with our wills when it wasn't, that God was real and good. We promised each other that we would make the appropriate response, which, of course, is faith.

By faith, Abraham put his son on the altar, believing that God was loving and trustworthy, even when he appeared to have lost his mind. He gave up once and for all the notion that he, as a mortal, could judge almighty God's righteousness. He gave up any claim to control God, or even understand him, and walked in terrified faith into the darkness of total obedience.

That was where God had placed us, and we were going to follow the path of Abraham. Of all the things in the world I dread, being separated from Beverly is at the top of the list, but if our marriage has to go on the altar, so be it. We will not question God's right to demand it, we will not demand that he explain it. He is God; we are not. When God demands sacrifices, the only sane thing to do is obey. Regardless of how it looks on the surface, God's intentions are always for our good, and if I have to leave Beverly behind, I am leaving her in the hands of my most trustworthy friend.

We promised each other that these were the principles we were gong to live by. Almost instantly, it was as though a crushing weight was lifted off our shoulders. Our frightened, selfish distrust of God had brought us to the edge of the pit of hell, and we had gotten a good look. Neither of us ever wants to go there again.

And neither of us ever has to.

> God moves in a mysterious way
> his wonders to perform:
> he plants his footsteps in the sea,
> and rides upon the storm.
>
> Deep in unfathomable mines,
> with never failing skill,
> he treasures up his bright designs,
> and works his sovereign will.
>
> Ye fearful saints, fresh courage take;
> the clouds ye so much dread
> are big with mercy, and shall break
> in blessings on your head.

Judge not the Lord by feeble sense,
but trust him for his grace;
behind a frowning providence
he hides a smiling face.

His purposes will ripen fast,
unfolding every hour:
the bud may have a bitter taste,
but sweet will be the flower.

Blind unbelief is sure to err,
and scan his work in vain;
God is his own interpreter,
and he will make it plain.

— *The Hymnal 1982.*
Words by William Cowper,
1731–1800

A Strange and Reckless Trust

Sometimes when I tell people that trusting God is what unlocks the power of Christianity, I get a rather bitter response. "Why should I trust God? Trusting God has never yet gotten me what I want. Look at the way my life has turned out. What about it should make me want to trust God?"

We need to be much clearer about what kind of trust we are talking about.

Jesus' earthly ministry includes a two-part lesson in trusting God. The first part is easy. The second is less so.

Particularly in the beginning, Jesus' ministry is dedicated to proving that his God is the most "human" of all gods, in the sense that he absolutely understands what makes people happy. At Cana, God shows that he not only understands the joy of a good party, but understands human tastes well enough to pick out a really good wine. He understands our intense desire to be healed when we are sick, and our joy when the healing comes. He understands the joy of an intimate evening with friends in Bethany. He understands how we enjoy the beauty of flowers. He understands the joy of having sympathetic friends around you when you are hurting. Jesus proves that, when God wants to make us happy, he knows us well enough to do a very good job of it.

The second lesson is more difficult. Jesus also presents us with the God of the cross. He knows what makes us happy, but for some reason he refuses to do it. He points us to our cross and tells us that the happiness we are looking for is on the other side of it, and then says, "Trust me."

This makes the trust God is asking for very different from the trust we usually want to give. We would like a God who gives us what we want for happiness, on our terms and according to our timetable, and then when he has established a track record, he can have our trust. The promise he makes is that whatever happens in life, when we reach the end of the story and can see what God was up to from his point of view, taking into consideration our present life, our eternal life, and how our life affects other people along the way, we will say (probably with a chuckle), "But that is just what I really wanted all along, even though I didn't know it. How did you know, Lord?"

This is trust that puts a frightening amount of control in God's hands, and very little in ours. We like to think,

"I should be in control, because I know what I want and after all it is *my* life." On the contrary, God would say, "You usually don't know what you want. You very often make yourself miserable with bad choices, and, incidentally, it is not your life."

Not my life? I know this will be one of the hardest ideas in this book to sell. But think a minute. What have you contributed to your life that gives you a claim to own it? You did not design your body or mind. You did not pay for the materials. You invested no labor in its construction. As far as you were concerned, your life just sort of appeared and you were somehow in it. What about any of this implies ownership?

It is amazing how much easier life becomes when I give up the idea that it is "my life." It gives me a lot of hope that the real owner (God) is far more skilled in managing it than I am.

Beverly discovered this when we moved to Peekskill. She had been happy in her job as organist and choir director of a good-sized Episcopal church on Long Island, and she was not happy about leaving. She used to say, "Jeff, I know God is calling you to Peekskill, but I don't think he has much for me up there. There are nothing but small churches with electronic organs and small choirs — nothing where I can use my training." Coming to Peekskill felt like a kind of death, a meaningless waste of everything she had worked hard for, but she believed she saw God's hand in it, and she didn't resist.

Two and a half months later, Bev got a call that an Episcopal church north of us had just lost its organist. A parishioner there was daughter-in-law to one of our permanent residents at the convent and called as soon as she heard. Bev went to see the rector and almost immediately had the job. Now she has the best pipe organ she has ever had, an adoring twenty-eight-voice choir, a wonderful boss, and (frankly) — if I were to die in the near future — one of the most loving parish communities I ever saw to make her home in. Letting God control her life rather than trying to do it herself has produced magnificent results.

The benefits of trusting God may not be as immediately obvious. Some may not be discernible at all this side of death. But I have seen this kind of trust rewarded repeatedly, and I am confident the principle is solid. Both Beverly and I intend to live that way as completely as we can.

⚭ ⚭ ⚭

When I am counseling other people on the subject of trusting God, I notice that each person starts with a set of assumptions — God is trustworthy, or he isn't. This book is primarily written for those who doubt God's trustworthiness but don't want to stay in that frame of mind. I want to outline some of the experiences that have been helpful to me.

If I am going to trust God, that involves trusting him to do something tangible. When the collection agency is phoning, a God who is only into ethereal blessings isn't going to meet my need. Many people have trouble trusting because they have so separated God from the material world that they can't imagine God interfering with their checkbook or their health.

One of my first experiences with God doing something I could actually see was during my first year of curacy right out of seminary. A woman in the parish was suddenly struck with a life-threatening case of ulcerative colitis. She was taken immediately to the hospital, where she weighed in at eight-seven pounds. Up until then she had been a vigorous person of normal weight. The doctors wanted to do surgery but were afraid that, given her condition, she would not survive it.

I went to the hospital to visit, armed with my reserved sacrament and oil stock and Prayer Book. We had a nice visit, and I said all the "right" prayers. At the end I was a little irritated when she asked a favor. "Here is the name of a priest on the North Shore, who has the reputation of a healing ministry. Would you mind giving him a call and asking him to come visit?"

Would I mind? I had done everything a priest was supposed to do. What more could this character have to offer?

But, of course, I made the call. The priest came almost immediately. Within a couple of days, she was showing improvement. A week later she was well on the road to recovery, and in two weeks, she was discharged. That was about twenty-seven years ago, and she was (at least until I lost touch with her) totally symptom-free.

To me, the shocking thing was the brute physicality of the thing. God was in Brookhaven Hospital, and whether you believed or not, you could not deny what your eyes were telling you.

My prayers had done, as far as evidence was concerned, virtually nothing. My colleague's prayers had given life to a virtually dead person. My conclusion: God had the power if I had the right attitude. It is a lesson I have seen repeated over and over, and it is significantly reinforcing my trust.

There are those who will object, "It was just a coincidence." I agree, although whenever I hear that, I respond with the famous squelch by Archbishop William Temple, who observed that "when I pray, coincidences happen; when I don't, they don't!"

TIP #10 FOR
SURVIVING HOSPITALS

Demand visits from the pastor of your church. Don't play the "I didn't tell him I was in the hospital — he should have just known" trick. Most clergy flunked mind reading in seminary.

Ten

Choosing Your Chair

"Here it is, Ladies and Gentlemen! From the nice people who brought you the padded cell and the straitjacket, the . . . (drum roll increases in volume) . . . Chemo-chair!"

Here we have the first piece of furniture that I believe was designed entirely by lawyers. Their job description was simple: "Create an environment that makes the patients totally safe, while unobtrusively taking away their control over everything."

When I went for my first dose of chemotherapy, it seemed enough like a normal chair. It has a nice headrest (something I insist on in real chairs), and armrests, and aside from its little wheels and handles sticking out the back at strange angles, it seemed chairlike enough.

Then the nurse attached the highchair table. No kidding. It is a little table shaped exactly like the one on a two-year-old's highchair that attaches into the armrests with heavy duty metal tubes two feet long. My first question is, "How do I get this off if I want to?" The answer, "You can't. You have to ask us to do it for you." My quietly muttered response, the only possible response of a former student of the University of Illinois Engineering College: "In a pig's eye. Just turn your back, brother."

In any case, it was home for the next four hours.

◕ ◕ ◕

First, there is the routine of "accessing the port," with a needle inserted in my chest. My first bag of medication (an anti-nausea drug) is attached, and I am free to explore my new three-foot-square environment.

As a design, it is perfect for its intended use. It is instantly cleanable if a patient does something unmentionable. It presents no sharp corners. The wheels are far too small for the patient to gain access and cause it to move. Thick panels on the sides guarantee that even the most confused patients will not do anything inappropriate with the patients next to them.

This chair is my enemy, and in this war I am not going to be defeated.

Having studied the Constitution and the Declaration of Independence, I recognize the most egregious violation of my basic God-given rights — the highchair table. As restraints go, it does the job as admirably as any set of handcuffs, but sooooo discretely.

I now understand why two-year-olds throw their oatmeal on the floor and take such delight in watching it go *splat.* With so much of your basic liberty taken away so suddenly and unobtrusively, it is a matter of honor to exercise whatever freedom of action you still have. And oatmeal means power. I start imagining the Statue of Liberty holding the torch of freedom in one hand and a bowl of really gooey oatmeal in the other. Maybe to celebrate the land of the free, on New Year's Eve in Times Square, they could drop, instead of the usual glass ball, a massive, five-hundred-gallon bowl of. . . .

Get a grip on yourself, Simmons. You don't have a bowl of oatmeal, and you are at war. Soldiers in critical situations must focus on the task at hand. It's okay. Everything you are planning is permitted under the Geneva Convention.

The latch releases are under the highchair table, about three inches in from the edge. The configuration of the room, where similar chairs are parked side by side with no clearance between, means that reaching outside the boundaries of the chair will accomplish nothing. Any successful assault must be an inside job.

There is room, for a fairly emaciated person like me, to slip my hands under the table. After some blind exploration, I grasp the two handles that spell freedom. Then the full diabolical genius of the designers of the chemo-chair becomes apparent. The table will yield only when both latches are simultaneously being pulled downward, with significant force. But now that the latches have yielded, and the table is free to blow off in a mild wind, you have no part of your anatomy left to push. The slight recline of the seat patronizingly pushes your torso against the backrest and away from your goal. Release either handle, to free a hand to push, and the table locks itself back into position.

The key is to position your upper body against the table before pulling the latches. Pull gently, and the little force you can apply will push the pins just past the locking holes. Once you have gotten that far, the table can be removed with no difficulty. Slip the metal tube into the armrest from the outside, and everything will look perfectly normal.

I put my newly liberated body in a number of unorthodox positions to celebrate my freedom. Then I notice I am under observation. The nurses aren't angry, just anxious. The routine has been broken. Where will it end?

Well, they can't watch me all day, and I haven't decided where it will end. But I am hot with the flush of success, and the spirit of Thomas Jefferson is stirring in my veins.

I love reclining chairs, but the idea of asking a college-trained registered nurse to recline the back of my chair just seems ridiculous. I think I remember — from seeing one of these things in the hospital — that the release is a horizontal bar in the back.

It is a very strange contortion. With your arm straight out behind you and your chest as close to the right edge of the chair as possible, slip your hand down the side looking for the fabled "fulcrum lever." Try not to think of Indiana Jones and the Temple of Doom. No daggers will come flying at you from hidden recesses in the walls if you make a false step. Your hand touches something promising, and you pull. Nothing happens. It is just a support beam.

Continuing downward into the invisible reaches. Another horizontal bar. You pull and it moves! A distant clanking sound greets your ears, and with a sullen creak, the footrests start to rise. Two nurses are at my side in a second. The look in their eye says they have just snatched a small child away from the brink of Niagara Falls. "Would you like your chair-back moved for you?"

I want to shout, "No. I just want to be treated like an adult human being." But they wouldn't understand, and I give in. I can afford to give in, because now I have The Secret.

At the end of the session, one of the nurses, who really is a good guy, says to me, "You don't have to do all this yourself. We are happy to do it for you. Here you are an honored guest."

Sometime I want to sit down with him and try to explain the emotional impact of these symbols of help-lessness. People who feel in control of their lives can gracefully accept being "honored guests." For people whom the medical establishment is surrounding with equipment like the chemo-chair, the feeling inevitably deteriorates from "honored guest" to helpless victim. I am not yet a helpless victim, and I will resist anything that seems to cast me in that role. It is a part of fighting for my life.

Somehow I can't help comparing the chemo-chair to another chair I sat in about six years ago. It was a much flimsier chair, so small that I could imagine my knees touching my chin. It was the pilot's seat in a Cessna 152, and for the first time in my life, I was the only one in the airplane. My instructor had just gotten out of the plane after saying, "After you have flown around the traffic pattern once and landed, pick me up here."

In that chair, everything I did mattered. Lack of con-centration or faulty judgment could kill. In fact, when I was turning on Runway 18, I almost did get tangled up with another Cessna that was making a straight in (and illegal) approach, and flew right over my head with not enough clearance for comfort. I arrived back where I had left my instructor, flushed, with my pulse racing, but totally invigorated and intensely alive.

In life we have to choose our chairs carefully.

In my line of work, I am often asked, reproachfully, "Why does God allow us to live in a world with so many dangers?"

I usually respond by asking, "If God gave you a perfectly safe world, would you like it?" Think carefully. If every time you wanted to take a walk in the woods, a supernatural voice told you, "You can't take the trail you were planning, because it has cliffs you might fall off," would you like it? If every time you wanted to join a bike race, or date a guy you didn't know, or climb a mountain, or canoe a river, or take a job with an exciting start-up company, something stopped you saying, "That's risky. You are not allowed to do it," how would you feel?

Some people think a perfectly safe world would be like heaven. I think it would be like the chemo-chair. I don't want any part of it.

I refuse to believe that I was put in this world to be safe. I was put in this world to *live*. Life has something to do with my actions having consequences for good or bad. Life has something to do with overcoming obstacles, with the possibility of heroism, nobility, growth in courage. Life is about putting on your armor and striking out into the trackless forest to rescue damsels and find the Holy Grail. Without that, or some variation of it, life is not worth living.

We have raised our son this way, and sometimes people get really mad at us. At the age of fifteen, he got a job bussing tables in a restaurant and announced he was saving money for pilot training. We encouraged him every way we could. Yes, we knew it was dangerous. On his long cross-country solo, he had a radio go dead on him as he was approaching Martha's Vineyard airport. He tried to land at one airport in Connecticut while he was in radio contact with another one. He hit a duck at forty-five-hundred feet crossing back over Long Island Sound and came back with a duck feather Scotch-taped to the back of his log book. But, dang it, he was alive, and he felt the sense of accomplishment and victory that makes life worthwhile.

If we had told him, "Son, flying airplanes is too dangerous, so we won't let you do it," we would have killed something precious and God-given within him. Our son now flies F-16s for the Air Force, and has flown numerous missions over Iraq. It is still dangerous, but it is still life-giving. We wouldn't change a thing.

Why does God put us in a world where there are so many dangers? I don't know, but if God is crazy, he is no crazier than all the people in my family. Human nature seems to need danger. Those who spend their lives avoiding it and complaining at God for making life so dangerous end up (in my experience) looking back at meaningless and depressing lives. It is as though they had spent their entire existence in chemo-chairs. Well, they were warned....

> For whoever wants to save his life will lose it, but whoever loses his life for me and for the gospel will save it.
> —Mark 8:35

What kind of chair are you sitting in?

The nursing supervisor has told me that "patients' rights" is
now the big thing. Apparently, someone has decided that my
roommate's right to play his television as loud as he likes (and
some hospital bed speakers can make the windows rattle)
supersedes my right to sleep, even in the middle of the night.
Hospitals used to maintain a library-like silence, but no more.
Your best course of defense is to build your own cone of si-
lence. If you have ever taken flying lessons, you probably have
an aviator's radio headset in the back of your closet. Take
it. If not, get the best set you can get your hands on. I have
a set of David Clark's. No sound gets through David Clark
headsets. If you throw the wires over the edge of the bed,

people will just assume you have a CD player. What you will hear is blissful, contemplative silence. But please note, most home stereo earphones have very little sound insulation, and are just not up to the challenge.

P.S.: Be patient with the nurses as they try to adjust to your new Halloween costume. (See Tips #9 and #13 on how to accessorize with eyeshades and judo outfit.) One of my nurses said, "You look like some kind of Martian." The thought of establishing communication with this "thing" in the bed leaves them a little anxious. You can judge a hospital worker's character by how he or she overcomes this hurdle. One night I was blissfully resting, and I felt this warm, firm grip clasp my hand. It was my oncologist, with a big smile on his face as though he was thoroughly enjoying the joke. Again, that was a moment of real bonding.

Eleven

Being Carried

My spiritual director gave me a piece of wonderful advice just after I was diagnosed. She said, "When you can't pray, let yourself be carried on the prayers of your friends." It sounded good at the time, but I had no idea how important it would become.

The chemo brought a week of severe diarrhea, and as I write this, I am in the hospital for a few days of rehydration. This morning I invented a game. I set the timer on my watch for one minute, start it, and then try to pray about one thing for a whole sixty seconds, without my mind wandering. At the moment, I am about 50 percent successful. It is humiliating.

The chemotherapy has made concentration almost impossible, so I have been doing what little I can and trusting the prayers of my friends to carry me.

I even make a little game of that (I believe it is permissible to regress in hospitals, so I don't apologize for playing all these games). I lie in the bed, get comfortable, and say, "Okay, guys, hoist me up."

The communion of saints — living and dead — is a really wonderful thing, especially when you start to think of them as personal friends.

And Then
There Are Angels

Some of the most intriguing accounts of God's activity involve angels. One of my favorites comes from a couple in my parish who were planning for retirement. They came to me one day looking a little shell-shocked, asking for guidance. During prayer, they had independently come to the conclusion that God was offering an invitation. They had been homeowners long enough for the thrill to have worn off. What did I think of their selling their home and using half the proceeds to set themselves up for serious Christian ministry?

After I stopped gasping, I admitted the idea had a good deal of merit. Very shortly the house went on the market.

The couple had figured out carefully how much the house would have to sell for in order for everything to work out. After several months, there were no offers, and they wondered if they had heard incorrectly.

They were tempted to lower the price and scale back the ministry.

One day the woman was praying intensely (and expecting an answer): "Lord do you want us to stand firm on the price or lower it?" There was a knock at the door, and when she answered it she saw a Long Island Lighting Company truck parked in the driveway with two workmen. They explained that the wires were getting tangled in the trees in the backyard and that they needed to prune some branches.

At that point, the conversation took a strange turn. One of the men asked her, "What were you doing just now?" That was an inappropriate question from the workman, but for some reason, it didn't strike her as particularly odd. He just seemed to inspire confidence, so she answered without hesitation, "Our house is on the market, and I was asking God if we should stand firm or lower the price." Instantly the repairman responded, "Stand firm and don't even think about lowering it." It was only after she had closed the door and gone back to praying that she realized what a bizarre conversation that really was.

They decided not to lower the price, and the house sold a short while later, giving them all the financial resources they needed. It was the beginning of a fruitful ten-year ministry.

Oddly, those power company workmen left without bothering to trim the branches in the backyard that day.

⟁ ⟁ ⟁

Most of the time, angels leave very subtle calling cards behind, so that you don't really know if you have dealt with an angel or not. They have been doing it for at least three thousand years, so they are very good at it.

Case in point: In 1995 Beverly and I took a sabbatical to Alaska. Part of it was study, and part of it was unapologetic vacation. We drove the Alaska Highway (all of it) and loved every minute. The trip was particularly nice because Matt was able to get leave time and join us for about three weeks, during which time we did a backpacking trip into Denali Park and canoed a 130-mile section of Birch Creek (only in Alaska would a body of water 250 miles long be called a "creek").

Denali Park, which contains Mount McKinley, is a section of land about the size of Massachusetts. Divided into twenty-four huge areas of jurisdiction, the park is very carefully managed to give backpackers the most authentic wilderness experience possible. All camping for backpackers is done by permit only, and only two camping permits are issued for each of the twenty-four areas. Needless to say, the population density of campers is extremely low.

We applied for our permit after having checked the map the night before and making a list of ten of the most desirable sites. The ranger informed us that all of them were taken. She offered us another site, which we had eliminated because the first mile and a half of land was marked "Off Limits to Backpackers." We decided to follow the "any old port in a storm" theory and signed up for two nights.

On our arrival, we ran into a ranger who asked us, "How did you know to choose the best area of the park?" I told him it was pure dumb luck, and I asked what made that section so desirable and why some of it was off limits. Both questions apparently had the same answer. He grinned cheerfully and said, "It has the highest concentration of grizzly bears in the park!" Then he wished us a great trip, and off we wandered into an area the size of two or three counties.

Our path to the tent site we had chosen led us through a heavily overgrown creek bed. Much to Matt's disgust, I insisted on following park regulations and made enough noise that a grizzly would hear us coming a good distance away (you never, never want to give a bear the impression you are sneaking up on him). Of course, after a while you run out of intelligent things to say, so you revert to dumb things like, "Watch out, bears. You are dealing with New Yorkers, and you don't want to tangle with them."

I felt I could get away with a little levity because there shouldn't have been any other human being within ten miles. But sure enough, just as I was at my silliest, a hiker came around the bend.

Although later we had a bit of trouble describing him, what we all remembered was that he was unusually tall and muscular, and had an air about him that was extremely attractive...the kind of guy you immediately want to have as your friend. We passed the usual small talk, and then he told us, "If I were you, I would get up on that ridge. There is a mother bear with two cubs just down the trail, and you are a lot safer if you are higher up."

He continued his way down the trail, and we got up on the ridge as fast as we could. It wasn't long before we spotted the bears and were very grateful to be where he had suggested. A face-to-face meeting could have been nasty. (Incidentally, as of 1995, Denali had never had a grizzly-bear-attack fatality — the result of the tight control and education of visitors the park authorities insist on. All of this is not as dangerous as you might suppose.)

Beverly pointed out the incongruity of all this when she asked, "Could that have been an angel?" My first reaction was to deny it. Why wasn't it just another encounter with a perfectly normal hiker? Then I started thinking about the probabilities.

- The population density was so low as to make an encounter with anyone very unlikely.

- He had been coming from the one direction where he could have learned the information we needed to hear.

I decided that in that setting the chances of meeting a human being were about equal to meeting an angel.

Am I sure about this? No. But I do know that leaving you in doubt about whether your new contact is human or angelic is definitely part of the angels' modus operandi, and has been for thousands of years.

☖ ☖ ☖

Learning to trust God comes from making one decision, "Do I want to trust God, and will I start acting like it?"

This is not like any scientific experiment. The results here will depend powerfully on your initial assumptions. The two principles are these:

> If anyone chooses to do God's will, he will find out whether my teaching comes from God or whether I speak on my own.
> — John 7:17

> Then he touched their eyes and said, "According to your faith will it be done to you."   — Matthew 9:29

Both of these verses state clearly that your experiment will conclusively prove one of two things: either God is trustworthy enough to give your life to, or untrustworthy to the point of being absent. It all depends on whether you really want to be obedient to him, and whether you start with whatever faith you can muster. You control the outcome!

My contention is that for those of us who want a trusting relationship with God and start with the right attitude, the proof will become so abundant that we will eventually no longer be able to close our eyes to it even if we wanted to. This is actually the way a lot of science works. Many scientists never make important discoveries because the idea seems so preposterous that they don't give it a second thought. Sixty-atom carbon molecules were the subject of hostile derision for quite some time until someone proved he had made some. Now they are taken for granted. So we are not being as unscientific here as it first appears.

Many people start with an angry, almost indestructible certainty that God is absent, malevolent, arbitrary, or involved in some unspeakable cat-and-mouse game with us. With that attitude and with the Lord's injunction "According to your faith..." they almost invariably reach the end of their life seeing no proof of anything different than they expected. Some people give God a tentative faith, and often they grow into people of powerful faith. Some people, unfortunately, imagine themselves as too pious to get mad at God with that kind of honesty, so they hide their anger and refusal to really believe under a cloak of conventional religious behavior. They remain conventional church members to the end, but what their real status with God is can only be conjectured.

Trust is not something that just lands on you, barring a special gift of grace. You make it happen by your decisions.

Twelve

Do You Want to Get Well?

When you're living with a diagnosis of cancer, some-times some strange thoughts run through your head.

I was at the dentist for a check-up and cleaning. He took some X-rays, and they showed some decay in an impacted wisdom tooth in my lower jaw. I was given the name of an oral surgeon and told bluntly that the tooth could really cause problems if I didn't have it taken out.

Then I heard a quiet, strangely comforting voice in the back of my mind saying, "You have cancer. You won't live long enough to have to worry about this. Isn't that nice?"

I have had a number of experiences like this — too many. I have been used to going through life dealing with problems as they come because I didn't have a choice. Now that I have the cancer, there is always a choice. The voice in the back of my head reminds me that dying can solve all kinds of problems. If I have to go on disability — and eventually can no longer get health insurance — death will solve that nicely. If one day I have to find another job but can't because no church will want to hire me with my medical history ... death can handle that one too.

TIP #12 FOR
SURVIVING HOSPITALS

Be aware when weight loss is making it possible for rings (especially wedding rings) to fall off. Mine has been an inseparable part of me for thirty years, but now this is becoming an issue.

So the worries pile up, getting more and more disconnected from reality — and death just sits there smiling and saying, "You don't have to deal with any of it."

I never used to understand how people could find not dealing with any of it attractive. Now I do. And knowing how seductive it can be, I am starting to realize how hard I have to fight against it.

One of the things that makes it most difficult is my tendency, when I am feeling sick, to assume I will feel sick for the rest of my life. On the other hand, when I am feeling good, I do not believe that I will feel good for the rest of my life. The fact is that neither the times when I feel good or bad tell me anything about how I am going to feel tomorrow. But assuming the worst can seriously sap my will to live, and I can't afford that.

Most people who have written about surviving cancer agree that survival requires a desire to live. I cannot control my emotions, and I can't force a desire to live, but I can make a conscious decision that I will do everything possible to live and not die. Ultimately, it is more a matter of acting than of feeling. But finding the necessary motivation, when your stomach is in an upheaval and all you want is to nap for the next three days, is much more difficult than people who have not experienced it would expect.

If I am going to conquer this particular demon, I will need help. I think I may be speaking for a good many other cancer patients when I say, I don't need lectures, guilt trips, or pep talks. I need a real listening ear, someone who can enter into the pain with me, and love me in spite of it.

I learned this in Pastoral Care 101, over thirty years ago. But in a real sense, I am only learning it now. I learned the theory then. I am coming to appreciate its power only now.

Thirteen

The Little Church That Wouldn't Let Go

The phone rings. "Hello?"

"Hi, it's your only friend."

"Hi, Greg."

Greg was a parishioner in my old parish, and one of the few who had kept in touch on a regular basis. (There is a reason for that, and it is my fault, as will become clear later.) I was particularly enjoying the relationship, because I no longer had to play the role of "Rector of the Parish." Instead, we could relax and be two regular guys enjoying each other's company, and that was neat.

Greg's message was that a good-sized group of people from the parish were going to drive up to Peekskill in a couple of weeks to pray with me for healing the cancer. I don't remember it being an offer. It was presented as an accomplished fact, and I wasn't being asked what I thought of the idea.

"Look, Jeff, if you needed to cut the cord when you left, that was a professional decision, and we respected that. But now you are in trouble. You need us, and we are your family, and *there is no way you are going to get rid of us!*"

There it was, I thought, with more than a pang of guilt. The Gospel I had been preaching there for twenty-two years was being preached back to me.

I felt a wild mix of emotions. I was amazed and thrilled that so many people (it turned out to be twenty-five) were willing to give up a whole Saturday and drive two hours each way to do this for me. The hunger to see my folks again was deep. Alongside this were some real feelings of guilt.

Not long before moving to Peekskill, I had attended an intense week-long seminar in parish administration. Now, parish administration experts sometimes preach from a different Gospel, one that says: "When you leave your parish, especially if you have been there a long time, make a clean break." The point, which I think is valid as far as it goes, is that the new rector has to be free to be the rector without the ghost of the old rector interfering. A former rector who continues to interfere in the life of a parish can destroy the ministry of the new person coming in.

My problem wasn't the basic idea so much as the absolutist way it was presented. It seems to be part of a "professionalization" of the priesthood that is being imposed on us more and more forcefully by the national church. The motive is fear of clergy-misconduct lawsuits, which have been increasing in number alarmingly over the last ten years. The national church's response has been to preach a detached, distant, and emotionally unconnected model of parish ministry. There was even a joke circulating among the clergy that the Church Insurance Company had developed a "safe ministry" kit, consisting of an enormous bell jar and a CB radio.

The priest, we are told, is a member of the diocese, but not a member of his own parish. He is not to have close friends in the parish. He is not to look to parishioners to meet his emotional needs. His relationship is basically all give and no take. He is to listen sympathetically to their problems, but not share his. He is to be available to them, but never to the point of becoming deeply emotionally involved. One poster I saw at a seminar went so far as to graph "pastoral effectiveness" as a function of "emotional detachment." The implication seemed to be that a priest was most "pastorally effective" when his emotional involvement was so low that he didn't really care if the parishioner he was talking to dropped dead at his feet.

And of course, once he left his parish, all personal relationships had to be severed. There had to be a "clean break."

The model, of course, assumed a priest's role was essentially the same as a modern psychotherapist, but seemed to have little to do with the way the Saints had been practicing Christian ministry over the last two millennia. Over the years, I think I made a bit of a reputation around the diocese saying so.

The relationship of a priest to his congregation, it seems to me, is intended to model God's relationship to his people. The core of the Gospel is that God loves — he becomes passionately, emotionally involved, and promises that his love will last forever.

> God has said, "Never will I leave you; never will I forsake you." —Hebrews 13:5

The great hope of Christians is that God's love is unconditional. You can't lose it by sin, and you don't need to fear he will lose interest and abandon you. God is making each of us a safe place where we don't need to worry if we are good enough to be there. Just wanting to be in God's "safe place" is the only requirement.

A Christian congregation is called to mirror God's unconditional love. The greatest biblical image of Christian community is not a group of friends. It is not even brothers and sisters in a family, although that imagery does appear in Scripture and would be plenty powerful even if that was all we had. The radical image of Christian community, which as far as I know has no parallel in any other human literature, is that Christians are related to each other like organs in a body. In St. Paul's wonderful metaphor, Christians can be (and should be) wildly different from each other, but joined by a bond so intimate that breaking fellowship should be as inconceivable as a person ripping off his own left arm!

TIP #13 FOR
SURVIVING HOSPITALS

Take your own pajamas and bathrobe, or even, if it makes you feel better, your own judo outfit. Hospital gowns are tremendous morale busters.

With this background, imposing the behavior and mindset of a psychotherapist on a parish priest is a profound step backward. Throughout Christian history, the church described the leader of a Christian community, whether parish or monastery, not as an outside professional, but as a "father" or "mother." Fatherhood and motherhood are marked by an intense emotional involvement in the life of the children, by open communication and intimacy, by a desire for the children's good, and by a willingness to guarantee the child's well-being even, if necessary, to the point of accepting death. The love of a parent for a child never ends — no matter what. To say that a father is not a member of his own family, or that a mother's effectiveness in mothering depends on her not getting emotionally involved with her child, is simply insane.

I think this is an insanity that is threatening our churches under the guise of "professionalism."

Over the years, in our own blundering way, we at Christ Church had tried to live the biblical model of Christian community. We developed a reputation as one of the most exuberantly affectionate congregations in the diocese. People shared their hurts so openly that we found we needed to put boxes of Kleenex in every third pew.

I had always considered the parish my family. I offered ministry when my people needed it, and I asked for ministry from them when I needed it, and they always responded with understanding and generosity. I kept almost no personal secrets from them, and they generally responded in kind.

Then, after all that time of doing it right, at the end I got suckered into doing it wrong. In obedience to a trendy modern theory, I had sent my congregation the message that my love for them had ended. However well intentioned, my behavior was contrary to the Gospel. They knew it, and they weren't going to let me get away with it. They knew they were standing on more solid theological ground than I was, and I knew it too.

So, I repented.

I remember that Saturday as one of the happiest of my life. We hugged, we cried a little, we sang and prayed and shared a meal.

And I got my family back.

Another group from the parish came up to visit several months later. If my cancer makes it necessary, I suspect I haven't seen the last of them either.

But for me the lesson is clear. Christianity is not about the latest church administration theories. Christianity is, and always has been, about love — simple, intense, permanent, reliable, and profoundly healing love. I should know. It healed me.

Fourteen

Involuntary Compassion

If only I had had these experiences when I was thirty. It would have changed my whole ministry in hospitals. It would even have changed my experience of the world in general.

It is easy to talk about "suffering" as though it were an experience like any other, until you've had a dose of the real thing. And yet, while I have had moments of feeling really rotten, there has never been a time when I could not imagine feeling worse, and I knew that other people were feeling exactly that at exactly that moment. While I have always known enough not to dispense glib platitudes on the subject, I now can imagine having the pain of a tumor blowing my liver up and trying to tear apart other internal organs. I can imagine living in a country where the nearest pain medication is two hundred miles away and costs ten years' salary. I can imagine having my pain, and having my parents reject me and leave me to die in a ditch — I recently heard a story from Africa like that. I can imagine feeling that death is imminent and not knowing what was going to happen after (for instance, I wouldn't relish the prospect of meeting up with the deities whose statues we once saw on a mission trip to Nepal).

TIP #14 FOR
SURVIVING HOSPITALS

Don't be afraid to ask your friends to pray for you. It is your

RIGHT as a member of the Christian community, and their

prayer can be very powerful.

When we are feeling good, we can make bad jokes that show we haven't understood anything. I woke up at 1:30 one night in the hospital and heard my room-mate's TV blaring: "Experience the most intense pain in television history. Can you survive The Chamber?"

But when you are really uncomfortable, pain is not an abstraction. The feelings physically attack you, like the electrocardiogram electrodes that won't come off without taking your hair and some of your skin with it. Or maybe like a bad meal you should be able to vomit up but can't. They leave you wondering, "Why couldn't I enter more into the pain of the person I met last week? Couldn't I have found something more comforting to say? Why did the suffering of the poor not touch me more powerfully?"

O God, forgive me for not caring more! O Jesus, when you bore our griefs, it must have been hideous. How in the name of heaven could I have been so ungrateful? Forgive me.

This is what judgment will really be like. I will see my hard-heartedness with no blinders, filters, and, with Jesus standing there, no possibility of rationalization. Jesus, I imagine, will be standing there, not with anger, but with tears, and it will hurt.

In that hour, dearest Lord, protect me from total disgust at myself. Grant me to stand in your presence and not to run away. You know how strong the temptation will be. Please don't let anything snatch me.

☙ Homily ☙

Bearing the Right Crosses

A book by Robert Barron, a Roman Catholic theologian, makes a powerful statement that may solve a problem I have had for over thirty years.

> Christian theology and spirituality come together in affirming that "either/or" tends to be the language of sin and "both/and" the language of grace.... The Great Tradition wants less clarity, less confidence, precisely because it sees theological murkiness and spiritual imbalance as conducive to the surrender that we in the dysfunctional family of Adam and Eve find so difficult.
> — Robert Barron, *And Now I See*

The "Great Tradition" of Christianity insists that we often have to believe two apparently contradictory things at the same time. How, for example, can we make logical sense of the claim that Jesus Christ was, at the same time, totally God and totally human? You can't, as many great minds have pointed out. Or how can God be all-powerful, but display his power in the weakness of a newborn baby in a manger?

Christian theology sometimes looks like too many ideas crammed into too small a box. In fact, one could almost argue that heresy is an attempt to make the Gospel neater by leaving out some of the ideas that don't seem to fit. In response, the church has always insisted on holding on to all the essential ideas, living with the apparent contradictions, and allowing for — sometimes even celebrating — the messiness.

We need the contradictions. To have to believe something that goes beyond logical sense is a powerful and necessary reminder that we don't know everything and we can't control everything. It is only when we are willing to admit our ignorance and powerlessness that we are willing to get out of the way and let God be God.

☙ ☙ ☙

I would like to apply this principle to the question of healing. Does God heal in response to our prayers? Over the years, the church has produced at least two different schools of thought on this, and the controversy between them has often been intense and angry. Perhaps if we get away from "either/or" thinking and try to see the issue in terms of "both/and," we might discover something valuable.

The first school of thought seems to have been pretty much unchallenged up until 1960 or so. In this view, God was not seen as a healer, but rather as a sender of "crosses," including illness. A cross sent from God was to be welcomed as a powerful aid to spiritual growth. The eighteenth-century Jesuit Jean-Pierre de Caussade has always seemed to me a particularly attractive proponent of this point of view.

> There is no moment at which God does not present himself under the guise of some suffering, some consolation, or some duty. All that occurs within us, around us and by our means covers and hides his divine action. . . .
>
> The will of God has nothing but sweetness, favors and treasures for souls submissive to it; we cannot have too much confidence in that will, we cannot abandon ourselves too much to it. God's will desires and can always accomplish what will contribute most to our perfection on condition that we allow God to act. Faith does not doubt this. The more our senses are faithless, revolted, uncertain and in despair, the more surely faith says: "This is God; all is well."
>
> — Jean Pierre de Caussade,
> *Self-Abandonment to Divine Providence*

It would be easy in the present theological climate to ridicule this position, but I am not going to. The joy and peace that leap out of the page when I read de Caussade is just too authentic. Whatever my disagreements with him, the man is a saint and has something important to say. However, if we let his theology stand on its own without some correctives, I think it has some fatal problems.

- It implies, and sometimes states outright, that God directly causes all disease, hardship and tragedy.

- It is impossible to reconcile this with Jesus' own attitude toward sickness and his aggressive healing ministry.

- It ignores the reality of supernatural evil.

- In the past it has produced massive pastoral problems and hurt a great many people.

The other viewpoint rose out of the Pentecostal and Charismatic renewal movements and began to influence the mainline churches in the 1960s. It looks to the example of Jesus' earthly ministry and proclaims him as an aggressive healer. It points out that in all the biblical accounts of Jesus' ministry, he never refused to heal anyone who came and asked for it. He seemed to assume that sickness was an evil, and he attacked it whenever it presented itself. Jesus never told anyone (as far as we know from Scripture) that God had sent a disease to someone for that person's spiritual betterment. In addition to his own healing ministry, Jesus had commissioned the Apostles to heal, and he seemed to assume that healing would always be a prominent feature of his church.

Catherine Marshall states this position compellingly:

Jesus said that He had come to earth to reveal His Father's nature and will to man. Then what was God's attitude towards sickness and disease as reflected in Jesus? I found that He placed any deviation from health in the same category as sin:

He saw both as the work of an evil force, both as intruders in the Father's world.... At the beginning of His ministry, He declared an all-out offensive against sin, disease, and death. Practically speaking, that meant that Jesus' attitude toward sickness was exactly that of any doctor today: He fought it all the way.

Nowhere in the gospel could I discover any hint of retreat or compromise in this position against disease. Jesus never refused to heal anyone who came to Him for help. He reproved every question of His willingness or His inability to heal. Never once did He say, as we so often do, "If it is God's will to heal...." For Him there were no *ifs* about His Father's will....

I could find no record of Jesus implying that an individual's spiritual state or the Kingdom of God would be furthered by ill-health. Not once did He say that sickness is a blessing....

Clearly it was Jesus' desire that we be rid of disease. What was his plan for achieving this? He said that faith in His Father's willingness and ability to give His children all good gifts was the key. In His eyes there was no evil that faith could not vanquish, no need that faith could not supply.

— Catherine Marshall, *Beyond Our Selves*

This seems a much more positive and optimistic approach. I am personally much more attracted to it. Still, in its pure form, it has serious problems familiar to anyone who has ever ministered to people in times of serious illness.

- It implies that the right kind of prayer, prayed with enough faith, should always lead to healing. In fact, no one, including the people of this century with the most legendary healing gifts, has been able to heal everyone who came to them.

Katherine Kuhlmann, Francis MacNutt, and John Wimber have all sent people home from healing services unhealed. In fact, many of the leaders in the healing ministry had poor health themselves!

- Once the position that "God always wills healing" has been accepted, sick people who don't experience healing can be put in an intolerable emotional position. Either they embark on an endless search for the "right" minister of healing, or the "right" kind of prayer, or they put massive effort into developing the "right" kind of faith. In a number of instances, I have in fact seen this kind of frantic searching lead to the healing the person desired. In many other cases, however, the healing is not forthcoming, and the sick person is plunged into terrible disillusionment and guilt. "If God always is willing to heal, and I haven't been healed, then either God isn't real after all, or there is something terribly wrong with me."

- This approach can see no redemptive value in suffering and gives people no hope or positive guidance when suffering seems to be unavoidable.

- There are certain biblical passages this approach can't account for, such as St. Paul's "thorn in the flesh" (2 Corinthians 12:7–9), a condition from which Paul prayed to be delivered repeatedly, but which God allowed to continue "to keep me from being too elated."

While the two schools of thought seem diametrically opposed to each other, is there any way we can reconcile the best of both viewpoints in a way that is spiritually satisfying if not necessarily totally logically consistent? This will be a very big job, and it will require better minds than mine to come up with the final word, but I will offer the following beliefs of mine at least as conversation starters.

- The notion that God is the cause of evil events like disease, accidents, and the like should be rejected out of hand as totally contrary to Jesus' example. God wants us to see him as "our refuge and strength, an ever present help in trouble" (Psalm 46:1), someone we can go to without fear, trusting that he will give "good gifts to those who ask him" (Matthew 7:11). He does not want us to think of him as the cause of our troubles.

- To explain the mess the world is in without blaming it all on God, we must take both human and supernatural evil seriously. Those who do not believe in the devil, it seems to me, are doomed to make God into a devil in his place.

- In any situation of illness, it is far better to assume that God's will is for healing, and to pray with boldness and persistence.

- It is the experience of anyone who has been part of a Christian community, however, that people of intense faith, who have no apparent barriers to healing and who are supported by vast networks of intercessory prayer, do often suffer from chronic, unhealed diseases, or even die from them. Much as I don't like it, I feel that I am being driven to the conclusion that sometimes it is not God's will to cure. My friend Nigel Mumford, who uses the words "cure" and "heal" carefully, says, "Through prayer, everyone is healed and some are cured."

- Even when healing comes, it may come slowly and be proceeded by a good deal of suffering. When all the appropriate prayers have been said and all the spiritual barriers to healing dealt with, it seems only logical and humane to assume that God somehow has chosen to permit this suffering.

- While our healing is not yet complete, unavoidable pain and weakness should be accepted as "our cross," not in the sense that God is inflicting it on us, but in the sense that in some mysterious way and for reasons of his own, God has not yet chosen to free us from it. In these cases, all the wisdom of de Caussade, Bishop Fenelon, etc., about bearing our cross lovingly, trustingly, and faithfully, should be brought to bear. We should in no way respond with angry accusations at either God or ourselves.

- If all this seems logically messy and unsatisfying, refer to the Robert Barron quote above (p. 126).

⚜ ⚜ ⚜

I am coming to see cross-bearing as an art, and a frequently misunderstood art. Knowing which crosses we should bear and which we should drop into the nearest ditch is at the center of the cross-bearer's art.

I have known people who pile self-inflicted misery on themselves, uncritically label all their unhappiness "my cross," and then present their martyr complex to the world as a proof of holiness. I know a man whose parents and religious instructors had inflicted this view on him. He used to say, "When I was a child, it was made very clear to me, 'God put you in this world to *suffer!*' " He had believed for years that the only reason he was alive was to gain the spiritual benefits of suffering — that life was intended to be an uninterrupted process of cross-bearing. Understandably, his rage against God was a major spiritual obstacle for years.

I believe that much of the cross-bearing we do, or maybe I should say, much of the cross-bearing I have done, was not in obedience to God, but in direct disobedience to him. Most of the time that we are bearing a cross, if we listened to God carefully, we would hear him yelling, "Put it down! Go out and enjoy the flowers!" Bearing the wrong crosses not only does us no good, but it robs us of the joy and power of bearing a real cross when it comes.

The first principle of the cross-bearer's art is this: "Never waste energy bearing a cross of a suffering that is in the future."

How many times have I tortured myself unnecessarily because I didn't follow this rule. I have known a good deal of misery in my life. I have experienced the bankruptcy of a church I was pastoring; I have been fired from my job; I have gone on welfare; I have experienced homelessness — and all of it, painful as it was, was totally imaginary! My parish did have difficult financial moments, and times when we had to put off paying some bills. I have had my parish treasurer say grimly, "Our finances are not in good shape this month." I have worried over loss of income when large contributors left the parish for one reason or another.

That was all reality. But then my imagination took over and made it infinitely worse than it was. (If you try to tell me you have never done this, I will probably not believe you.) Nights when I can't sleep are the worst. Tossing in bed around 3:00 a.m. I can convince myself that the most preposterous disaster scenarios are almost certain to happen. So I bear my cross, and it weighs me to the ground, robs me of my happiness, and makes me a particularly poor example to the outside world of what Christian freedom and joy are supposed to be all about.

God gives me no help in bearing these crosses. They are actually sin, direct violations of clear commands that God has given. Jesus makes it clear that indulging in worry about the future is both forbidden and stupid. "Fear not" is the most frequently repeated command (not "invitation," but "command") in the whole Bible. Jesus drives his point home most forcefully in what is, unfortunately, probably the most ignored and discounted passage in all Scripture:

> "Therefore I tell you, do not worry about your life, what you will eat or drink; or about your body, what you will wear. Is not life more important than food, and the body more important than clothes? Look at the birds of the air; they do not sow or reap or store away in barns, and yet your heavenly Father feeds them. Are you not much more valuable than they? Who of you by worrying can add a single hour to his life? And why do you worry about clothes? See how the lilies of the field grow. They do not labor or spin. Yet I tell you that not even Solomon in all his splendor was dressed like one of these. If that is how God clothes the grass of the field, which is here today and tomorrow is thrown into the fire, will he

not much more clothe you, O you of little faith? So do not worry, saying, 'What shall we eat?' or 'What shall we drink?' or 'What shall we wear?' For the pagans run after all these things, and your heavenly Father knows that you need them. But seek first his kingdom and his righteousness, and all these things will be given to you as well. Therefore do not worry about tomorrow, for tomorrow will worry about itself. Each day has enough trouble of its own."   — Matthew 6:25–34

Years of preaching on this passage, and getting re- actions at parish coffee hours, have convinced me that most Christians see it as a beautiful, utopian sentiment, given by Jesus to decorate religious greeting cards. Jesus, on the other hand, is obviously setting this out as the only ultimately practical and responsible foundation for a healthy life.

When I look back over the years, I often ask, "At what points has God ever failed to come through on his promise? When have my needs not been met?" The answer is that, while I thought it was going to happen any number of times, it never happened once! I believe we have tried, timidly and inconsistently, to be sure, to seek God's Kingdom first, and he has always been there for us. Based on my past experience, I can see that he has earned my total trust, and I would be a fool (which I often am) not to give it to him.

I would suggest the second rule of intelligent cross- bearing is this: "Never bear a cross if the suffering is the cause of bad decisions you have made that are within your power to change."

It must make God sad, and a bit irritated, to watch us shoot ourselves in the foot and then point to the bullet hole and say, "This is a cross God inflicted on me." I know an architect who found himself unemployable because he couldn't bring himself to learn the Computer-Aided Design programs that had made his beloved drafting board and pencils obsolete. I have known intelligent people who trapped themselves in low-paying, menial jobs because they wouldn't face the fact that their interpersonal skills were so poor that nobody could stand to work in the same office with them.

But then, once all that is said, there are still crosses. They are here, right now, and nothing can be done to make them go away. They are ugly and they have your name written all over them. Now what?

        ⚅ ⚅ ⚅

There is something to be said for planned, deliberate cross-bearing, so let's make a cup of tea, sit down in a comfortable chair, and do the best job of this we can.

I will take my crosses, just as an example. Today I am home taking one of many sick days, because I still haven't recovered my strength from last week's hospitalization.

The first thing to be clear about is that my cancer is not my cross, if I mean the whole disease, start to finish. I never experience "my cancer" as a whole. Much of it — the initial fear after being told the diagnosis, the needle biopsy, the recovery from surgery — is in the past where it can't hurt me anymore, so I can forget it. Reminding myself of that can be a relief just in itself. The parts of the disease in the future — being disabled; the discomfort that comes when the chemo doesn't work anymore and the tumors are out of control; whatever death I end up dying — are forbidden territory. God has said, "Don't worry about it," and so I can indulge in the luxury of not worrying about it. That is also a comfort.

The only part of the cancer that is my cross is what it is doing right now. When I focus exclusively on the present, I find a dull ache in my stomach, exhaustion, and frustration at the things I want to do, but can't. That is today's cross, and it is real. Tomorrow's cross may be heavier, but this one has enough weight to practice on.

One advantage of taking time to deliberately bear my cross is the pleasant discovery that my real cross is much lighter than I thought. (I must take some time to praise God for that.)

But I am still stuck at home with a throbbing stomach, and I don't like it much.

So I start to bear my cross by reminding myself that my pain and frustration are not meaningless. The world thinks of sick time as wasted time, useless time, and if you are sick too much, it makes you a worthless person. If we follow St. Paul's lead, time spent in sickness and pain is filled with spiritual opportunity. Right now, lying on my back with my body hurting and my thoughts fogged up, I may well accomplish the most important things of my life!

The Abbé de Tourville expresses this beautifully in one of his letters of spiritual direction:

> So as I have told you (and I believe my experience may help my friends) after two years of uncertainty, of illness, of being laid aside, of patient waiting, I find myself achieving results which I would not have hoped for after years of active work and energetic study.... Yes, suffering is a potent force...and is no less than one of the great motive powers controlling the movement of this world towards eternity.
> —Henri de Tourville, *Streams of Grace*

I can make my suffering a potent force by handing it back to God in prayer. Even when I hurt, I can still pray. If I fall asleep, I can pray again when I wake up. In my prayer, I put myself in agreement with whatever he is doing in my life. I give him permission to change me any way he wants. I praise him for what he is doing. As much as possible, I make myself soft, malleable clay in his hands, and I trustingly leave him to do the rest.

I can offer myself as an intercessor. I can quietly ask God to bring to mind anyone who particularly needs prayer. I can let my mind range, remembering recent natural disasters in Africa, the guerrilla war in Indonesia, the newborn who isn't eating properly, the acquaintance in need of a job. I have known people who developed such powers as intercessors that it is easy to imagine them changing world history right from their beds.

Done properly, cross-bearing is a sacrament of trust in God, a time of joy in cooperating with the divine, mixed with the thrill of almost infinite possibilities. I think it is worth the effort to learn to do it right.

Fifteen

Entering Heaven

I once had a fantasy, or a daydream, or something, about what it would be like to enter heaven. I think I was wide awake when it happened, probably in a setting where I should have been paying attention to something else. Still, the fantasy came and seemed to have a life of its own.

I imagined entering heaven like waking up from a very pleasant night's sleep, drowsy, relaxed, and feeling very safe. Gradually I become aware of music. My guardian angel, who happens to be a soprano (if yours isn't, you have my sympathy, but mine is) is singing one of the most heartbreakingly beautiful solos in all choral music, the "Laudate Dominum" from Mozart's *Solemn Vespers*. The sound is very pure, angelic rather than human, lacking the voluptuousness that all human voices have to some degree, but with a bloodless, silvery quality perfectly suited to the music.

"Laudate Dominum omnes gentes." The singer is issuing a joyful invitation to all the races and peoples of the earth to praise God.

I listen, charmed and relaxed, wanting nothing else but that the music will last forever. Suddenly I am jerked wide awake and my heart skips several beats, or maybe stops entirely when I realize where this is all leading. I almost feel like the victim of an impish practical joke. In any case, I have only seconds before I have to make a momentous decision.

The music is moving inexorably to a point where a full four-voice chorus will join in — and I know the bass part!

But the music is perfect when sung just by angels. It is beyond belief that I, raspy-voiced baritone with no vocal experience except community choruses and church choirs, am really being invited to launch my less than perfect voice into the midst of all this perfection.

But Mozart has written this piece so that the soprano can't achieve her artistic destiny unless supported by the chorus. I have no way of knowing, but if I don't sing, will there be any bass part at all? If I do sing, won't I ruin it all? Or has God arranged things so that even the angels need me, in my gross, earthbound humanity, to join in his praise in order to have the fullness he wants?

The downbeat for the chorus — my downbeat — is only seconds away. I am torn between intense desire and intense panic. I am awestruck at the honor being offered to me and panic stricken that I will turn something sublimely beautiful into something blasphemously ugly.

At the last moment, I do the only possible thing. I open my mouth and, in a moment of joyful recklessness, I sing. Only then do I become aware of a line of huge thunderclouds almost directly overhead. The sound I hear is my voice, but my voice, resonating off the clouds, somehow merges with their thunder, a thousand times more powerful and vibrant than my voice has ever been before. I am singing in a real chorus, and the thunderclouds are my fellow basses. In fact, they couldn't sing at all until I led them. I can feel creation aching to praise God but unable to do it without my lead. Because I am human, I am the section leader. Indispensable in spite of my flaws.

TIP #15 FOR
SURVIVING HOSPITALS

Have a project. For example this book is my project. Yours could be an afghan for a grandchild, or a set of letters to family members about what you have learned in life. It drives away a sense of hopelessness and keeps your mind on something. A wise priest told me recently that this book might be helpful to others, but it was also very healing for me personally. How right he was.

TIP #16 FOR
SURVIVING HOSPITALS

Like everyone else, nurses and nurse's aides react well to ordinary friendliness and less well to hostility and criticism. Use this as an opportunity to make friends, and it will pay dividends.

Sixteen

My Pregnancy

Today, I became unmistakably pregnant. If I stand sideways to the mirror, put my hands under my swollen abdomen, and look at myself, I bear a passable resemblance to those fashion magazine ads designed to make pregnancy look stylish. My condition may be delicate, but believe me, there is nothing stylish about it.

My favorite aunt, when she was fighting cancer, used to go to the doctor for a procedure that drew the fluid out of the abdomen and gave her about two weeks of relief each time. I will ask my oncologist about it. It will mean more needles, but I should be used to them by now.

It is a shock when the disease starts leaving marks on your body that are visible from twenty feet away. Up till now, I could blame it on gas, or chemo, but now I am pretty sure it's the cancer.

I have just started chemo again after a break of seven weeks. The oncologist said — and I agree — that without a break, the chemo would be more of a threat to my survival than the cancer. Nevertheless I have had my first chemo treatment of the new cycle, and I can hope it will start shrinking the tumors and restoring liver function.

So I am not dying. Not yet. But as my son said about his most recent posting in the Air Force, "It is not the end of the world, but you can see it from here."

This isn't the end of my life. Not yet. But I can see it from here. Lying in bed awake about midnight and imagining what the end will be like, I can honestly claim a more accurate view of it than I could before this happened.

❦ ❦ ❦

As I imagine it (the time just before death), I am with my father, and we are enjoying poems. They are the kind of poems that have no particular justification and that more business-like people would call a waste of time: poems where "terrible wolf" somehow transforms itself into "wearable tulf"(from one of my childhood favorites called *The Pee Little Thrigs*); poems where owls and pussycats on honeymoon eat with a "runcible spoon." (I ran a Google search on the Internet for "The Owl and the Pussycat," and the first page had two references linking the Pussycat with prostitution. And you think I am wasting *my* time!) Actually, there are some useful warnings and practical suggestions about living about which any father would be negligent if he didn't sternly warn his son. Since my dad warned me about them, I have always been very careful to shun the "frumious bandersnatch." (My copy of Microsoft Word is having a cow over the word "frumious." What does *it* know? We are in a world where strict grammarians and stuffy dictionary fundamentalists are not — and never will be — invited.)

What am I doing? I am being tutored, with the help of my dad, for the greatest examination of my life. My second-semester quantum mechanics final in college and the week-long "General Ordination Exams" in seminary were nothing compared to this.

This examination has only one question, and the grade is pass/fail: "Can you believe that someone else has done the studying for you, that he has taken the exam, passed with a perfect score, and is offering you his grade?"

I have had people tell me that this test is too easy. I usually answer, "It may be easy for you, but it wasn't easy for Him."

He had to make it easy for us. He wanted to make it easy, because there was no other test we could pass.

When a drowning man is being pulled out of the water by a lifeguard, his survival depends on his going limp and not doing anything. That's his test. If he is not willing to trust the lifeguard but insists that he do half the work himself and starts flailing and thrashing around, he will fail the test and drown.

> Every athlete exercises self-control in all things. They do it to receive a perishable wreath, but we an imperishable. Well, I do not run aimlessly. I do not box as one beating the air: but I pommel my body and subdue it, lest after preaching to others I myself should be disqualified.   — 1 Corinthians 9:25–27

At the moment, my pommeled body is doing a good job of subduing itself. It doesn't need much help from me. The great masters have always said that the best spiritual training consists of accepting, and cooperating joyfully and confidently with, the pommeling that life brings all by itself. I have taken on no special Lenten rule this year. I just want to live in a holy way with the cancer. I think the lesson I am learning is that my body is not the master of anything — a lesson I had not learned in my younger years.

I think a lot of clergy disqualify themselves for the prize. I used to joke that clergy firmly believe that lay people are saved by faith, but clergy are saved only by lots of good works. The compulsive drive to minister till we drop or end up hopelessly alcoholic is proof enough of that.

I have certainly been disabused of the idea that my body can do anything to save me. At the moment it can't do much of anything, period. It can only trust — or not.

> "Look here! This is how you must cultivate Christ in yourself, and see how in him God holds before you his mercy and offers it to you without any prior merits of your own. It is from such a view of his grace that you must draw faith and confidence in the forgiveness of all your sins. Faith therefore does not originate in works; neither do works create faith but faith must spring up and flow from the blood and wounds and death of Christ. If you see in these that God is so kindly disposed toward you that he even gives his own Son for you, then your heart in turn must grow sweet and disposed toward God. And in this way your confidence must grow out of pure good will and love — God's toward you, and yours toward God."
>
> — Martin Luther, *Treatise on Good Works*

You really can't improve on Martin Luther...so I won't try.

Seventeen

The Big Announcement

It seems that cancer, more than any other disease, divides itself naturally into separate phases, with a Big Announcement at the beginning of each phase. Beverly and I have just heard the last Big Announcement.

Dr. Friedman has just told us that he believes it is time to move from fighting the disease to focusing on keeping me comfortable. We are surprised but not surprised. It means we accept the end as close and essentially inevitable, barring the miracle for which we have been praying for the last eight months.

My main question is, "What happened to the optimism of the last four weeks?" The answer is that the change in blood markers has been far faster than anyone would have suspected. The bilirubin marker is so high as to automatically exclude me from any clinical trials. This cancer is just raging. Dr. Friedman says the speed of the cancer is just too explosive to make it treatable.

He actually isn't telling me anything I wasn't pretty sure of already. For the past two weeks, I have experienced an unmistakable deterioration. When I get out of bed at night and worry I am going to fall over, or when I open my mouth and am afraid I may not succeed in saying something intelligent (one of the blood tests says the level of ammonia in the blood is rising, and that makes you think in strange channels)... when all these things happen, I know it isn't just a bad cold.

To finally accept this is a great relief. I will keep fighting, but to feel that I have to force myself to eat when it makes me sick — I can give that up happily enough. To feel that I have to force myself to say mass for the sisters to prove I am not that seriously ill, well, I will not miss having to keep up the pretense. For Beverly and me, to feel we have to keep each other's chin up, using tire jacks if necessary, is robbing us of our chance to mourn together, and I won't miss it.

Every step in the direction of honesty is good.

Eighteen

For Better or Worse

Beverly and I took our wedding vows twice, first at the wedding ceremony itself, and second over a wonderful pot of cheese fondue (with the obligatory red wine and salad . . . the perfect romantic meal for impecunious seminarians).

I took her hand and said, "Too many people take these vows (because they have to) and then break them (because they never meant them in the first place). I promise you I will never abandon you. I will never divorce you. If tomorrow you suddenly go totally insane and don't even recognize me, and if you are that way for twenty years and then you suddenly are cured and discharged from the hospital, you will find me in the waiting room, ready to take you home. This is my solemn vow."

I guess I am a fanatic on unconditional love, but I can't imagine how a really solid marriage can be built on anything else, and neither can Bev. I have never had the experience of wondering if I would come home and find a "Dear John" letter on the kitchen table. It's been wonderful.

It boils down to a simple anthropological principle. Human beings are capable of making promises and keeping them. We gambled on that principle . . . and won!

The real benefits of this have been clear since the illness. When one is really helpless — and there have been some trying times — a spouse may need to do some unpleasant things. Mine smiles and says, "For better or for worse, in sickness and in health, right?" and I know she will be there.

And she is.

The Moment of Graduation

Beverly Simmons

"His blood pressure is eighty over zero." The hospice nurse has stopped in to check on my husband, who lies in the hospital bed in the living room. For the past twenty-four hours he has been unresponsive when I speak to him or hold his hand. Although his eyes are open some of the time I'm not sure he is really seeing. I stand on one side of the bed, his brother on the other.

So what does a blood pressure of eighty over zero mean? The nurse explains that he could die within a few hours or possibly not for a few more days. Some people are just so reluctant to give up that their reserves keep them going even at this point.

Jeff and I have had many conversations over the past months and especially the last few weeks since the doctor told him the chemo was not doing any good and we should get hospice care. Although ready to go and be

154

with the Lord, he has been reluctant to leave me. It was a long road during the last seven months for each of us to reach this point of acceptance. He has been kept comfortable with drugs as necessary and has no fear of dying. I am prepared — or am I? How do you ever say good-bye to your very best friend and your loving husband of thirty-one years?

And yet I don't want him to linger. We have both been in agreement on that. Ever since the diagnosis of colon cancer that was already in the liver, we have agreed that we would fight this thing as hard as we could, but when it was obvious that there was nothing more that could be done we would pray for a speedy death. So three weeks ago today when the doctor informed us that we had reached that point, we put out the word to our friends. We asked them to pray for a holy and peaceful death as quickly as possible.

I spend the morning at my desk only a few feet from the bed so I can watch for any change. Today is the Friday before Palm Sunday. I told him earlier in the week when he could still understand and laugh that I thought as a priest who is married to a church musician he ought to know better than to die during Holy Week. I have seven services to play from now through Easter plus a choir rehearsal before each service and an extra one during the week. Our rector is very understanding and knows I may not be able to do some or even all of these liturgies. But there is no back up plan and I don't want to leave the parish without music if I can help it.

So I sit at my desk going over the details of the funeral service which we planned together. It will have to be on a Saturday so that many of our friends will be able to drive the two and a half hours from Long Island to get to our parish in Wappingers Falls, New York. Jeff served in a parish in Port Jefferson, Long Island, for over twenty-two years, and we left only two years ago. Since the nurse is sure he will be dead within a few hours or at most a day or two that will mean a funeral on Holy Saturday. Is that possible?

I call our priest, who assures me that it is. Next I call the suffragan bishop of Long Island with whom Jeff spoke about ten days ago. I'll never forget listening in on that phone call when Jeff calmly told him that he was dying and asked if he would be willing to celebrate his funeral. So I check to be sure that he would be available that day and promise to get back to him. Next comes a call to the bishop of Albany to see if he can preach. Yes, he, too, is available then. Two bishops who are both available that day — that's a miracle in itself.

Enough phone calls. I go back to the bed and hold Jeff's hand. I talk to him and tell him that I love him and that he is free to go when it is time. I assure him with more courage than I feel that I will be all right. I love him very, very much but when God calls him home

I don't want him to hesitate. I get no response, not even a squeeze of the hand.

One of our cats, Dugal, is curled up by his feet. A few days ago when I tried to move him off the bed thinking it was bothering him, Jeff was emphatic that it was fine. So I leave Dugal in place. He definitely senses something is wrong and wants to be there.

Jeff's brother Steve and I eat lunch, and after the home health aide arrives we both go upstairs for a nap. I doubt that either of us slept, but it did feel good to lie down for a bit. The aide had instructions to call if anything changed.

When I came down a couple of hours later Steve was singing hymns to Jeff. I joined in on a couple and then let them have some time alone. About 4:30 Steve pointed out that he thought Jeff's breathing was really slowing down. At first I couldn't tell, but then it became obvious. As Jeff was taking his last breath at 5:00 p.m. I called our priest to come. The three of us gathered around the bed and said the prayers for the dying and the departed. After we finished we each turned away and began to cry. Jeff had graduated to eternal life. Such a beautiful life, such a holy death.